FIFTH EDITION

Python Pocket Reference

Mark Lutz

Beijing · Cambridge · Farnham · Köln · Sebastopol · Tokyo

Python Pocket Reference, Fifth Edition

by Mark Lutz

Printed in the United States of America.

Published by O'Reilly Media, Inc., 1005 Gravenstein Highway North, Sebastopol, CA 95472.

O'Reilly books may be purchased for educational, business, or sales promotional use. Online editions are also available for most titles (*http://safaribookson line.com*). For more information, contact our corporate/institutional sales department: 800-998-9938 or *corporate@oreilly.com*.

Editor: Rachel Roumeliotis
Production Editor: Kristen Brown
Copyeditor: Richard Carey
Proofreader: Amanda Kersey
Indexer: Lucie Haskins
Cover Designer: Randy Comer
Interior Designer: David Futato

October 1998:	First Edition
January 2002:	Second Edition
February 2005:	Third Edition
October 2009:	Fourth Edition
February 2014:	Fifth Edition

Revision History for the Fifth Edition:

2014-01-17:	First release
2014-02-14:	Second release
2015-02-06:	Third release

See *http://oreilly.com/catalog/errata.csp?isbn=9781449357016* for release details.

ISBN: 978-1-449-35701-6

[LSI]

Table of Contents

Python Pocket Reference

Introduction

Python is a general-purpose, multiparadigm, open source computer programming language, with support for object-oriented, functional, and procedural coding structures. It is commonly used both for standalone programs and for scripting applications in a wide variety of domains, and is generally considered to be one of the most widely used programming languages in the world.

Among Python's features are an emphasis on code readability and library functionality, and a design that optimizes developer productivity, software quality, program portability, and component integration. Python programs run on most platforms in common use, including Unix and Linux, Windows and Macintosh, Java and .NET, Android and iOS, and more.

This *pocket reference* summarizes Python types and statements, special method names, built-in functions and exceptions, commonly used standard library modules, and other prominent Python tools. It is intended to serve as a concise reference tool for developers and is designed to be a companion to other books that provide tutorials, code examples, and other learning materials.

This *fifth edition* covers both Python 3.X and 2.X. It focuses primarily on 3.X, but also documents differences in 2.X along the way. Specifically, this edition has been updated to be current with Python versions 3.3 and 2.7 as well as prominent enhancements in the imminent 3.4 release, although most of its content also applies both to earlier and to later releases in the 3.X and 2.X lines.

This edition also applies to all major implementations of Python —including CPython, PyPy, Jython, IronPython, and Stackless —and has been updated and expanded for recent changes in language, libraries, and practice. Its changes include new coverage of the MRO and super(); formal algorithms of inheritance, imports, context managers, and block indentation; and commonly used library modules and tools, including json, timeit, random, subprocess, enum, and the new Windows launcher.

Book Conventions

The following notational conventions are used in this book:

[]
> In syntax formats, items in brackets are optional; brackets are also used literally in some parts of Python's syntax as noted where applicable (e.g., lists).

*
> In syntax formats, items followed by an asterisk can be repeated zero or more times; star is also used literally in some parts of Python's syntax (e.g., multiplication).

a | b
> In syntax formats, items separated by a bar are alternatives; bar is also used literally in some parts of Python's syntax (e.g., union).

Italic
> Used for filenames and URLs, and to highlight new or important terms.

Constant width
> Used for code, commands, and command-line options, and to indicate the names of modules, functions, attributes, variables, and methods.

Constant width italic
> Used for replaceable parameter names in the syntax of command lines, expressions, functions, and methods.

Function()
> Except where noted, callable functions and methods are denoted by trailing parentheses, to distinguish them from other types of attributes.

See "Section Header Name"
> References to other sections in this book are given by section header text in double quotes.

NOTE

In this book, "3.X" and "2.X" mean that a topic applies to all commonly used releases in a Python line. More specific release numbers are used for topics of more limited scope (e.g., "2.7" means 2.7 only). Because future Python changes can invalidate applicability to future releases, also see Python's "What's New" documents, currently maintained at *http://docs.python.org/3/whatsnew/index.html* for Pythons released after this book.

Python Command-Line Usage

Command lines used to launch Python programs from a system shell have the following format:

```
python [option*]
    [ scriptfile | -c command | -m module | - ] [arg*]
```

In this format, *python* denotes the Python interpreter executable with either a full directory path, or the word python that is resolved by the system shell (e.g., via PATH settings). Command-line options intended for Python itself appear before the specification of the program code to be run (*option*). Arguments intended for the code to be run appear after the program specification (*arg*).

Python Command Options

The *option* items in Python command lines are used by Python itself, and can be any of the following in Python 3.X (see "Python 2.X Command Options" ahead for 2.X differences):

-b

    Issue warnings for calling `str()` with a `bytes` or `bytearray` object and no encoding argument, and comparing a `bytes` or `bytearray` with a `str`. Option `-bb` issues errors instead.

-B

    Do not write *.pyc* or *.pyo* byte-code files on imports.

-d

    Turn on parser debugging output (for developers of the Python core).

-E

    Ignore Python environment variables described ahead (such as `PYTHONPATH`).

-h

    Print help message and exit.

-i

    Enter interactive mode after executing a script. Hint: useful for postmortem debugging; see also `pdb.pm()`, described in Python's library manuals.

-O

    Optimize generated byte code (create and use *.pyo* byte-code files). Currently yields a minor performance improvement.

-OO

    Operates like `-O`, the previous option, but also removes docstrings from byte code.

-q

    Do not print version and copyright message on interactive startup (as of Python 3.2).

-s

> Do not add the user site directory to the sys.path module
> search path.

-S

> Do not imply "import site" on initialization.

-u

> Force *stdout* and *stderr* to be unbuffered and binary.

-v

> Print a message each time a module is initialized, showing
> the place from which it is loaded; repeat this flag for more
> verbose output.

-V

> Print Python version number and exit (also available as
> --version).

-W *arg*

> Warnings control: *arg* takes the form *action*:*message*:
> *category*:*module*:*lineno*. See also "Warnings Framework"
> and "Warning Category Exceptions" ahead, and the warn
> ings module documentation in the Python Library Refer-
> ence manual (available at *http://www.python.org/doc/*).

-x

> Skip first line of source, allowing use of non-Unix forms of
> #!*cmd*.

-X *option*

> Set implementation-specific option (as of Python 3.2); see
> implementation documentation for supported *option*
> values.

Command-Line Program Specification

Code to be run and command-line arguments to send to it are
specified in the following ways in Python command lines:

scriptfile

Denotes the name of a Python script file to run as the main, topmost file of a program (e.g., *python* main.py runs the code in main.py). The script's name may be an absolute or relative (to ".") filename path, and is made available in sys.argv[0]. On some platforms, command lines may also omit the *python* component if they begin with a script file name and have no options for Python itself.

-c *command*

Specifies Python code (as a string) to run (e.g., *python* -c "print('spam' * 8)" runs a Python print operation). sys.argv[0] is set to '-c'.

-m *module*

Runs a module as a script: searches for *module* on sys.path and runs it as a top-level file (e.g., *python* -m pdb s.py runs the Python debugger module pdb located in a standard library directory, with argument s.py). *module* may also name a package (e.g., idlelib.idle). sys.argv[0] is set to the module's full path name.

–

Reads Python commands from the standard input stream, *stdin* (the default); enters interactive mode if *stdin* is a "tty" (interactive device). sys.argv[0] is set to '-'.

arg*

Indicates that anything else on the command line is passed to the script file or command, and appears in the built-in list of strings sys.argv[1:].

If no *scriptfile*, *command*, or *module* is given, Python enters interactive mode, reading commands from *stdin* (and using GNU *readline* for input, if installed), and setting sys.argv[0] to '' (the empty string) unless invoked with option - in the preceding list.

Besides using traditional command lines at a system shell prompt, you can also generally start Python programs by clicking their filenames in a file explorer GUI; by calling functions in the

Python standard library (e.g., os.popen()); by using program-launch menu options in IDEs such as IDLE, Komodo, Eclipse, and NetBeans; and so on.

Python 2.X Command Options

Python 2.X supports the same command-line format, but does not support the -b option, which is related to Python 3.X's string type changes, nor the recent -q and -X additions in 3.X. It supports additional options in 2.6 and 2.7 (some may be present earlier):

-t *and* -tt

> Issues warnings for inconsistent mixtures of tabs and spaces in indentation. Option -tt issues errors instead. Python 3.X always treats such mixtures as syntax errors (see also "Syntax Rules").

-Q

> Division-related options: -Qold (the default), -Qwarn, -Qwarnall, and -Qnew. These are subsumed by the new true division behavior of Python 3.X (see also "Operator Usage Notes").

-3

> Issues warnings about any Python 3.X incompatibilities in code that the Python standard installation's *2to3* tool cannot trivially fix.

-R

> Enables a pseudorandom salt to make hash values of various types be unpredictable between separate invocations of the interpreter, as a defense against denial-of-service attacks. New in Python 2.6.8. This switch is also present in 3.X as of 3.2.3 for compatibility, but this hash randomization is enabled by default as of 3.3.

Python Environment Variables

Environment (a.k.a. *shell*) variables are systemwide settings that span programs and are used for global configuration.

Operational Variables

The following are major user-configurable environment variables related to script behavior:

PYTHONPATH

Augments the default search path for imported module files. The format of this variable's value is the same as the shell's PATH setting: directory pathnames separated by colons (semicolons on Windows). If set, module imports search for imported files or directories in each directory listed in PYTHONPATH, from left to right. Merged into `sys.path`—the full module search path for leftmost components in absolute imports—after the script's directory, and before standard library directories. See also `sys.path` in "The sys Module", and "The import Statement".

PYTHONSTARTUP

If set to the name of a readable file, the Python commands in that file are executed before the first prompt is displayed in interactive mode (useful to define often-used tools).

PYTHONHOME

If set, the value is used as an alternate prefix directory for library modules (or `sys.prefix`, `sys.exec_prefix`). The default module search path uses `sys.prefix/lib`.

PYTHONCASEOK

If set, filename case is ignored in import statements (currently only on Windows and OS X).

PYTHONIOENCODING

Assign to string *encodingname*[:*errorhandler*] to override the default Unicode encoding (and optional error handler) used for text transfers made to the *stdin*, *stdout*, and *stderr* streams. This setting may be required for non-ASCII text in some shells (e.g., try setting this to `utf8` or other if prints fail).

PYTHONHASHSEED

   If set to "random", a random value is used to seed the hashes
   of str, bytes, and datetime objects; may also be set to an
   integer in the range 0…4,294,967,295 to get hash values with
   a predictable seed (as of Python 3.2.3 and 2.6.8).

PYTHONFAULTHANDLER

   If set, Python registers handlers at startup to dump a traceback on fatal signal errors (as of Python 3.3, and equivalent
   to -X faulthandler).

Python Command Option Variables

The following environment variables are synonymous with some
of Python's command-line options (see "Python Command Options"):

PYTHONDEBUG

   If nonempty, same as -d option.

PYTHONDONTWRITEBYTECODE

   If nonempty, same as -B option.

PYTHONINSPECT

   If nonempty, same as -i option.

PYTHONNOUSERSITE

   If nonempty, same as -s option.

PYTHONOPTIMIZE

   If nonempty, same as -O option.

PYTHONUNBUFFERED

   If nonempty, same as -u option.

PYTHONVERBOSE

   If nonempty, same as -v option.

PYTHONWARNINGS

   If nonempty, same as -W option, with same value. Also accepts a comma-separated string as equivalent to multiple -W
   options. (As of Python 3.2 and 2.7.)

Python Windows Launcher Usage

On Windows (only), Python 3.3 and later install a script launcher, also available separately for earlier versions. This launcher consists of the executables py.exe (console) and pyw.exe (nonconsole), which can be invoked without PATH settings; are registered to run Python files via filename associations; and allow Python versions to be selected in three ways—with "#!" Unix-like directives at the top of scripts, with command-line arguments, and with configurable defaults.

Launcher File Directives

The launcher recognizes "#!" lines at the top of script files that name Python versions in one of the following forms, in which * is either: *empty* to use the default version (currently 2 if installed and similar to omitting a "#!" line); a *major* version number (e.g., 3) to launch the latest version in that line installed; or a *complete major.minor* specification, optionally suffixed by -32 to prefer a 32-bit install (e.g., 3.1-32):

```
#!/usr/bin/env python*
#!/usr/bin/python*
#!/usr/local/bin/python*
#!python*
```

Any Python (python.exe) arguments may be given at the end of the line, and Python 3.4 and later may consult PATH for "#!" lines that give just python with no explicit version number.

Launcher Command Lines

The launcher may also be invoked from a system shell with command lines of the following form:

```
py [pyarg] [pythonarg*] script.py [scriptarg*]
```

More generally, anything that may appear in a python command after its *python* component may also appear after the optional *pyarg* in a py command, and is passed on to the spawned Python verbatim. This includes the -m, -c, and - program specification forms; see "Python Command-Line Usage".

The launcher accepts the following argument forms for its optional *pyarg*, which mirror the * part at the end of a file's "#!" line:

```
-2          Launch latest 2.X version installed
-3          Launch latest 3.X version installed
-X.Y        Launch specified version (X is 2 or 3)
-X.Y-32     Launch the specified 32-bit version
```

If both are present, command-line arguments have precedence over values given in "#!" lines. As installed, "#!" lines may be applied in more contexts (e.g., icon clicks).

Launcher Environment Variables

The launcher also recognizes optional environment variable settings, which may be used to customize version selection in default or partial cases (e.g., missing or major-only "#!" or py command argument):

```
PY_PYTHON     Version to use in default cases (else 2)
PY_PYTHON3    Version to use in 3 partials (e.g., 3.2)
PY_PYTHON2    Version to use in 2 partials (e.g., 2.6)
```

These settings are used only by launcher executables, not when *python* is invoked directly.

Built-in Types and Operators

Operators and Precedence

Table 1 lists Python's expression operators. Operators in the lower cells of this table have higher precedence (i.e., bind tighter) when used in mixed-operator expressions without parentheses.

Atomic terms and dynamic typing

In Table 1, the replaceable expression items *X*, *Y*, *Z*, *i*, *j*, and *k* may be:

- *Variable names*, replaced with their most recently assigned value
- *Literal expressions*, defined in "Specific Built-in Types"
- *Nested expressions*, taken from any row in this table, possibly in parentheses

Python *variables* follow a *dynamic typing model*—they are not declared, and are created by being assigned; have object references as values, and may reference any type of object; and must be assigned before appearing in expressions, as they have no default value. Case is always significant in variable names (see "Name Rules"). *Objects* referenced by variables are automatically created, and automatically reclaimed when no longer in use by Python's *garbage collector*, which uses reference counters in CPython.

Also in Table 1, replaceable *attr* must be the literal (unquoted) name of an attribute; *args1* is a formal arguments list as defined in "The def Statement"; *args2* is an input arguments list as defined in "The Expression Statement"; and a literal ... qualifies as an atomic expression in 3.X (only).

The syntax of comprehensions and data structure literals (tuple, list, dictionary, and set) given abstractly in the last three rows of Table 1 is defined in "Specific Built-in Types".

Table 1. Python 3.X expression operators and precedence

Operator	Description
yield X	Generator function result (returns send( ) value)
lambda *args1*: X	Anonymous function maker (returns X when called)
X if Y else Z	Ternary selection (X is evaluated only if Y is true)
X or Y	Logical OR: Y is evaluated only if X is false
X and Y	Logical AND: Y is evaluated only if X is true
not X	Logical negation
X in Y, X not in Y	Membership: iterables, sets
X is Y, X is not Y	Object identity tests
$X < Y$, $X <= Y$, $X > Y$, $X >= Y$	Magnitude comparisons, set subset and superset
$X == Y$, $X != Y$	Equality operators
$X \mid Y$	Bitwise OR, set union
$X \wedge Y$	Bitwise exclusive OR, set symmetric difference
$X \& Y$	Bitwise AND, set intersection
$X << Y$, $X >> Y$	Shift X left, right by Y bits
$X + Y$, $X - Y$	Addition/concatenation, subtraction/set difference
$X * Y$, $X \% Y$, X / Y, $X // Y$	Multiplication/repetition, remainder/format, division, floor division
$-X$, $+X$	Unary negation, identity
$\tilde{}X$	Bitwise NOT complement (inversion)
$X ** Y$	Power (exponentiation)
$X[i]$	Indexing (sequence, mapping, others)
$X[i:j:k]$	Slicing (all three bounds optional)
X(*args2*)	Call (function, method, class, other callable)

Operator	Description
X.attr	Attribute reference
(....)	Tuple, expression, generator expression
[....]	List, list comprehension
{....}	Dictionary, set, dictionary and set comprehension

Operator Usage Notes

- In Python 2.X only, value inequality can be written as either *X* != *Y* or *X* <> *Y*. In Python 3.X, the latter of these options is removed because it is redundant.

- In Python 2.X only, a backquotes expression `` `X` `` works the same as repr(*X*), and converts objects to display strings. In Python 3.X, use the more readable str() and repr() built-in functions instead.

- In both Python 3.X and 2.X, the *X* // *Y floor division* expression always truncates fractional remainders, and returns an integer result for integers.

- The *X* / *Y* expression performs *true division* in 3.X (always retaining remainders in a floating-point result), and *classic division* in 2.X (truncating remainders for integers) unless 3.X's true division is enabled in 2.X with from __future__ import division or Python option -Qnew.

- The syntax [....] is used for both list literals and list comprehension expressions. The latter of these performs an implied loop and collects expression results in a new list.

- The syntax (....) is used for tuples and expressions, as well as generator expressions—a form of list comprehension that produces results on demand, instead of building a result list. Parentheses may sometimes be omitted in all three constructs. When a tuple's parentheses are omitted, the *comma* separating its items acts like a lowest-precedence operator if not otherwise significant.

- The syntax {....} is used for dictionary literals. In Python 3.X and 2.7, it is also used for set literals, and both dictionary and set comprehensions; use set() and looping statements in 2.6 and earlier.

- The yield and ternary if/else selection expressions are available in Python 2.5 and later. The former returns send() arguments in generators; the latter is a shorthand for a multiline if statement. yield requires parentheses if not alone on the right side of an assignment statement.

- Comparison operators may be chained: $X < Y < Z$ produces the same result as $X < Y$ and $Y < Z$, but Y is evaluated only once in the chained form.

- The slice expression $X[i:j:k]$ is equivalent to indexing with a slice object: $X[slice(i, j, k)]$.

- In Python 2.X, magnitude comparisons of mixed types are allowed—converting numbers to a common type, and ordering other mixed types according to the type name. In Python 3.X, nonnumeric mixed-type magnitude comparisons are not allowed and raise exceptions; this includes sorts by proxy.

- Magnitude comparisons for dictionaries are also no longer supported in Python 3.X (although equality tests are); comparing sorted(adict.items()) is one possible replacement in 3.X.

- Call expressions allow for positional and keyword arguments, and arbitrarily large numbers of both; see "The Expression Statement" and "The def Statement" for call syntax.

- Python 3.X allows ellipsis (literally, ..., and known by built-in name Ellipsis) to be used as an atomic expression anywhere in source code. This may be used as an alternative to pass or None in some contexts (e.g., stubbed-out function bodies, type-independent variable initialization).

- Although uncertain at this writing, Python 3.5 or later *may* generalize the `*X` and `**X` star syntax to appear in data structure literals and comprehensions, where it will unpack collections into individual items, much as it currently does in function calls. See "The Assignment Statement" for more details.

Operations by Category

In this section, trailing parentheses are omitted from `__X__` method names for brevity. In general, all built-in types support the *comparisons* and *Boolean* operations listed in Table 2 (although Python 3.X does not support magnitude comparisons for dictionaries or mixed nonnumeric types).

Boolean *true* means any nonzero number or any nonempty collection object (list, dictionary, etc.), and all objects have a Boolean value. The built-in names `True` and `False` are preassigned to true and false values and behave like integers 1 and 0 with custom display formats. The special object `None` is false and appears in various Python contexts.

Comparisons return `True` or `False` and are automatically applied recursively in compound objects as needed to determine a result.

Boolean `and` and `or` operators stop (short-circuit) as soon as a result is known and return one of the two operand objects—the value on the left or the right of the operator—whose Boolean value gives the result.

Table 2. Comparisons and Boolean operations

Operator	Description
X < Y	Strictly less than[a]
X <= Y	Less than or equal to
X > Y	Strictly greater than
X >= Y	Greater than or equal to
X == Y	Equal to (same value)

Operator	Description
X != Y	Not equal to (same as X<>Y in Python 2.X only)[b]
X is Y	Same object
X is not Y	Negated object identity
X < Y < Z	Chained comparisons
not X	If X is false then True; else, False
X or Y	If X is false then Y; else, X
X and Y	If X is false then X; else, Y

[a] To implement comparison expressions, see both the rich comparison (e.g., __lt__ for <) class methods in 3.X and 2.X, and general __cmp__ method in 2.X, described in "Operator Overloading Methods".

[b] != and <> both mean not equal by value in 2.X, but != is the preferred syntax in 2.X and the only supported option in 3.X. is performs an identity test; == performs value comparison, and so is much more generally useful.

Tables 3 through 6 define operations common to types in the three major type categories—*sequence* (positionally ordered), *mapping* (access-by-key), and *number* (all numeric types)—as well as operations available for *mutable* (changeable) types in Python. Most types also export additional type-specific operations (e.g., methods), as described in "Specific Built-in Types".

Table 3. Sequence operations (strings, lists, tuples, bytes, bytearray)

Operation	Description	Class method
X in S X not in S	Membership tests	__contains__, __iter__, __getitem__ [a]
S1 + S2	Concatenation	__add__
S * N, N * S	Repetition	__mul__
S[i]	Index by offset	__getitem__

Operation	Description	Class method
S[i:j], S[i:j:k]	Slicing: items in S from offset i through j−1 by optional stride k	__getitem__[b]
len(S)	Length	__len__
min(S), max(S)	Minimum, maximum item	__iter__, __getitem__
iter(S)	Iteration protocol	__iter__
for X in S:, [expr for X in S], map(func, S), etc.	Iteration (all contexts)	__iter__, __getitem__

[a] See also "The iteration protocol" for more on these methods and their interplay. If defined, __contains__ is preferred over __iter__, and __iter__ is preferred over __getitem__.

[b] In Python 2.X, you may also define __getslice__, __setslice__, and __delslice__ to handle slicing operations. In 3.X, these are removed in favor of passing slice objects to their item-based indexing counterparts. Slice objects may be used explicitly in indexing expressions in place of i:j:k bounds.

Table 4. Mutable sequence operations (lists, bytearray)

Operation	Description	Class method
S[i] = X	Index assignment: change item at existing offset i to reference X	__setitem__
S[i:j] = I, S[i:j:k] = I	Slice assignment: S from i through j−1 with optional stride k (possibly empty) is replaced by all items in iterable I	__setitem__
del S[i]	Index deletion	__delitem__
del S[i:j], del S[i:j:k]	Slice deletion	__delitem__

Table 5. Mapping operations (dictionaries)

Operation	Description	Class method
D[k]	Index by key	__getitem__
D[k] = X	Key assignment: change or create entry for key *k* to reference *X*	__setitem__
del D[k]	Delete item by key	__delitem__
len(D)	Length (number of keys)	__len__
k in D	Key membership test[a]	Same as in Table 3
k not in D	Converse of *k* in *D*	Same as in Table 3
iter(D)	Iterator object for *D*'s keys	Same as in Table 3
for k in D:, etc.	Iterate through keys in *D* (all iteration contexts)	Same as in Table 3

[a] In Python 2.X, key membership may also be coded as D.has_key(k). This method is removed in Python 3.X in favor of the in expression, which is also generally preferred in 2.X. See "Dictionaries".

Table 6. Numeric operations (all number types)

Operation	Description	Class method
X + Y, X − Y	Add, subtract	__add__, __sub__
X * Y, X / Y, X // Y, X % Y	Multiply, divide, floor divide, remainder	__mul__, __truediv__[a], __floordiv__, __mod__
−X, +X	Negative, identity	__neg__, __pos__
X | Y, X & Y, X ^ Y	Bitwise OR, AND, exclusive OR (integers)	__or__, __and__, __xor__
X << N, X >> N	Bitwise left-shift, right-shift (integers)	__lshift__, __rshift__
˜X	Bitwise invert (integers)	__invert__
X ** Y	*X* to the power *Y*	__pow__
abs(X)	Absolute value	__abs__

Operation	Description	Class method
int(X)	Convert to integer[b]	__int__
float(X)	Convert to float	__float__
complex(X), complex(re,im)	Make a complex value	__complex__
divmod(X, Y)	Tuple: (X / Y, X % Y)	__divmod__
pow(X, Y [,Z])	Raise to a power	__pow__

[a] The / operator invokes __truediv__ in Python 3.X, but __div__ in Python 2.X unless true division is enabled. See "Operator Usage Notes" for division semantics.

[b] In Python 2.X, the long() built-in function invokes the __long__ class method. In Python 3.X, the int type subsumes long, which is removed.

Sequence Operation Notes

Examples and notes on selected sequence operations in Table 3 and Table 4:

Indexing: S[i]

- Fetches components at offsets (first item is at offset 0).

- Negative indexes count backward from the end (last item is at offset -1).

- S[0] fetches the first item; S[1] fetches the second item.

- S[-2] fetches the second-to-last item (same as S[len(S) - 2]).

Slicing: S[i:j]

- Extracts contiguous sections of a sequence, from i through j-1.

- Slice boundaries i and j default to 0 and sequence length len(S).

- S[1:3] fetches from offsets 1 up to, but not including, 3.

- S[1:] fetches from offsets 1 through the end (len(S)-1).

- $S[:-1]$ fetches from offsets 0 up to, but not including, the last item.

- $S[:]$ makes a top-level (shallow) copy of sequence object S.

Extended slicing: S[i:j:k]

- The third item k is a stride (default 1), added to the offset of each item extracted.

- $S[::2]$ is every other item in entire sequence S.

- $S[::-1]$ is sequence S reversed.

- $S[4:1:-1]$ fetches from offsets 4 up to, but not including, 1, reversed.

Slice assignment: S[i:j:k] = I

- Slice assignment is similar to deleting and then inserting where deleted.

- Iterables assigned to basic slices $S[i:j]$ need not match in size.

- Iterables assigned to extended slices $S[i:j:k]$ must match in size.

Other

- Concatenation, repetition, and slicing return new objects (though not always for tuples).

Specific Built-in Types

This section covers numbers, strings, lists, dictionaries, tuples, files, sets, and other core built-in types. Its subsections give details common to both Python 3.X and 2.X. In general, all the compound datatypes covered here (e.g., lists, dictionaries, and tuples) can nest inside each other arbitrarily and as deeply as required. Sets may participate in nesting as well, but may contain only immutable objects.

Numbers

Numbers are *immutable* (unchangeable) values, supporting numeric operations. This section covers basic number types (integers, floating-point), as well as more advanced types (complex, decimals, and fractions).

Literals and creation

Numbers are written in a variety of numeric literal forms, and created by some built-in operations:

1234, −24, +42, 0
: Integers (unlimited precision).[1]

1.23, 3.14e-10, 4E210, 4.0e+210, 1., .1
: Floating-point (normally implemented as C doubles in CPython).

0o177, 0x9ff, 0b1111
: Octal, hex, and binary literals for integers.[2]

3+4j, 3.0+4.0j, 3J
: Complex numbers.

---

1. In Python 2.X, there is a distinct type named long for unlimited-precision integers; int is for normal integers with precision that is usually limited to 32 bits. Long objects may be coded with a trailing "L" (e.g., 99999L), although integers are automatically promoted to longs if they require the extra precision. In 3.X, the int type provides unlimited precision and so subsumes both the 2.X int and long types; the "L" literal syntax is removed in 3.X.

2. In Python 2.X, octal literals may also be written with just a leading zero —0777 and 0o777 are equivalent. In 3.X, only the latter form is supported for octal.

```
decimal.Decimal('1.33'), fractions.Fraction(4, 3)
```
Module-based types: decimal, fraction.

```
int(9.1), int('-9'), int('1111', 2), int('0b1111', 0),
float(9), float('1e2'), float('-.1'), complex(3, 4.0)
```
Create numbers from other objects, or from strings with possible base conversion. Conversely, hex(N), oct(N), and bin(N) create digit strings for integers, and string formatting makes general strings for numbers. See also "String formatting", "Type Conversions", and "Built-in Functions".

Operations

Number types support all *number operations* (see Table 6 on page 19). In mixed-type expressions, Python converts operands up to the type of the "highest" type, where integer is lower than floating-point, which is lower than complex. As of Python 3.0 and 2.6, integer and floating-point objects also have a handful of type-specific *methods* and other *attributes*; see Python's Library Reference manual for details:

```
>>> (2.5).as_integer_ratio()          # float attrs
(5, 2)
>>> (2.5).is_integer()
False

>>> (2).numerator, (2).denominator    # int attrs
(2, 1)
>>> (255).bit_length(), bin(255)       # 3.1+ method
(8, '0b11111111')
```

Decimal and fraction

Python provides two additional numeric types in standard library modules—*decimal* is a fixed-precision, floating-point number, and *fraction* is a rational type that keeps numerator and denominator explicitly. Both may be used to address inaccuracies of floating-point arithmetic:

```
>>> 0.1 - 0.3
-0.19999999999999998
```

```
>>> from decimal import Decimal
>>> Decimal('0.1') - Decimal('0.3')
Decimal('-0.2')

>>> from fractions import Fraction
>>> Fraction(1, 10) - Fraction(3, 10)
Fraction(-1, 5)

>>> Fraction(1, 3) + Fraction(7, 6)
Fraction(3, 2)
```

Fractions automatically simplify results. By fixing precision and supporting various truncation and rounding protocols, decimals are useful for monetary applications. See the Python Library Reference for details.

Other numeric types

Python also includes a *set* type (described in "Sets"). Additional numeric types such as optimized vectors and matrixes are available as third-party open source extensions (e.g., see the *NumPy* package at *http://www.numpy.org*). The third-party domain also includes support for visualization, statistical tools, extended precision floating-point math, and more (see the Web).

Strings

The normal str string object is an *immutable* (unchangeable) *sequence* of characters accessed by *offset* (position). Its *characters* are code point ordinals in the underlying character set, and individual characters are string objects of length 1.

The full string object model varies across lines.

Python 3.X has three string types with similar interfaces:

str

> An immutable sequence of characters, used for all text— both ASCII and richer Unicode.

`bytes`

> An immutable sequence of short integers, used for the byte values of binary data.

`bytearray`

> A mutable variant of bytes.

Python 2.X instead has two string types with similar interfaces:

`str`

> An immutable sequence of characters, used for both byte oriented (8-bit) text and binary data.

`unicode`

> An immutable sequence of characters, used for possibly-richer Unicode text.

Python 2.X (as of 2.6) also has the Python 3.X `bytearray` type as a back-port from 3.X, but it does not impose as sharp a distinction between text and binary data. (It may be mixed with text strings freely in 2.X.)

For Unicode support in both 3.X and 2.X, see "Unicode Strings". Most of the remainder of this section pertains to all string types, but see "String methods", "Unicode Strings", and "Built-in Functions" for more on `bytes` and `bytearray`.

Literals and creation

String literals are written as a series of characters in quotes, optionally preceded with a designator character, and in all string literal forms an empty string is coded as adjacent quotes. Various built-in operations also return new strings:

`'Python"s', "Python's"`

> Single and double quotes work the same, and each can embed unescaped quotes of the other kind.

`"""This is a multiline block"""`

> Triple-quoted blocks collect multiple lines of text into a single string, with end-of-line markers (\n) inserted between the original quoted lines.

`'Python\'s\n'`
> Backslash escape code sequences (see Table 7) are replaced with the special-character code point values they represent (e.g., `'\n'` is an ASCII character with decimal code-point value 10).

`"This" "is" "concatenated"`
> Adjacent string constants are concatenated. Hint: this form may span lines if parenthesized.

`r'a raw\string', R'another\one'`
> Raw strings: backslashes are retained literally (except at the end of a string). Useful for regular expressions and Windows (DOS) directory paths: e.g., `r'c:\dir1\file'`.

`hex(), oct(), bin()`
> Create hex/octal/binary digit strings from integer numbers. See "Numbers" and "Built-in Functions".

The following literal forms and calls make specialized strings described in "Unicode Strings":

`b'...'`
> bytes string literal in Python 3.X: sequence of 8-bit byte values representing raw binary data. For 3.X compatibility, this form is also available in Python 2.6 and 2.7, where it simply creates a normal str string. See "String methods", "Unicode Strings", and "Built-in Functions".

`bytearray(...)`
> bytearray string construction: a mutable variant of bytes. Available in Python 3.X, and in Python 2.X as of 2.6. See "String methods", "Unicode Strings", and "Built-in Functions".

`u'...'`
> Unicode string literal in Python 2.X: a sequence of Unicode code points. For 2.X compatibility, this form is also available in Python 3.X as of 3.3, where it simply creates a normal str string (but normal string literals and str strings support Unicode text in Python 3.X). See "Unicode Strings".

str(), bytes(), bytearray() *(and* unicode() *in 2.X only)*
    Create strings from objects, with possible Unicode encoding/decoding in Python 3.X. See "Built-in Functions".

String literals may contain escape sequences taken from Table 7 to represent special characters.

Table 7. String constant escape codes

Escape	Meaning	Escape	Meaning
\newline	Ignored continuation	\t	Horizontal tab
\\	Backslash (\)	\v	Vertical tab
\'	Single quote (')	\N{id}	Unicode dbase id
\"	Double quote (")	\uhhhh	Unicode 16-bit hex
\a	Bell	\Uhhhhhhhh	Unicode 32-bit hex[a]
\b	Backspace	\xhh	Hex (at most 2 digits)
\f	Formfeed	\ooo	Octal (up to 3 digits)
\n	Line feed	\0	Null (not end of string)
\r	Carriage return	\other	Not an escape

[a] \Uhhhhhhhh takes exactly eight hexadecimal digits (h); both \u and \U can be used only in Unicode string literals.

Operations

All string types support all *sequence operations* (see Table 3), plus string-specific *methods* (described in "String methods"). In addition, the str type supports string *formatting* % expressions and template substitution (discussed next), and the bytearray type supports *mutable sequence operations* (Table 4, plus extra list-like methods). Also see the re string pattern-matching module in "The re Pattern-Matching Module", and string-related, built-in functions in "Built-in Functions".

String formatting

In both Python 3.X and 2.X (as of 3.0 and 2.6), normal str strings support two different flavors of string formatting—operations that format objects according to format description strings:

- The original expression (all Python versions), coded with the % operator: *fmt* % (*values*)

- The newer method (3.0, 2.6, and later), coded with call syntax: *fmt*.format(*values*)

Both produce new strings based on possibly type-specific substitution codes. Their results may be displayed, or assigned to variables for later use:

```
>>> '%s, %s, %.2f' % (42, 'spam', 1 / 3.0)
'42, spam, 0.33'

>>> '{0}, {1}, {2:.2f}'.format(42, 'spam', 1 / 3.0)
'42, spam, 0.33'
```

Although the method call seems to have evolved more rapidly in recent years, the expression is used extensively in existing code, and both forms are still fully supported. Moreover, although some view the method form as marginally more mnemonic and consistent, the expression is often simpler and more concise. As these two forms are largely just minor variations on a theme of equivalent functionality and complexity, there is today no compelling reason to recommend one over the other.

String formatting expression

String formatting *expressions* replace % targets in the string on the left of the % operator, with values on the right (similar to C's sprintf). If more than one value is to be replaced, they must be coded as a tuple to the right of the % operator. If just one item is to be replaced, it can be coded as a single value or one-item tuple on the right (nest tuples to format a tuple itself). If key names are used on the left, a dictionary must be supplied on the right, and * allows width and precision to be passed in dynamically:

```
>>> 'The knights who say %s!' % 'Ni'
'The knights who say Ni!'
>>> '%d %s, %d you' % (1, 'spam', 4.0)
'1 spam, 4 you'
>>> '%(n)d named %(x)s' % {'n': 1, 'x': "spam"}
'1 named spam'
>>> '%(n).0E => [%(x)-6s]' % dict(n=100, x='spam')
'1E+02 => [spam  ]'
>>> '%f, %.2f, %+.*f' % (1/3.0, 1/3.0, 4, 1/3.0)
'0.333333, 0.33, +0.3333'
```

Formatting expression syntax

In the format string on the left of the % operator, substitution targets have the following general format, all but the last component of which is optional (text outside such substitution targets is retained verbatim):

%[(keyname)][flags][width][.prec]typecode

In this substitution target syntax:

keyname

References an item in the expected dictionary, in parentheses.

flags

Can be - (left-justify), + (numeric sign), a space (use a blank before positive numbers and a - for negatives), and 0 (zero fill).

width

The total minimum field width (use * to fetch from values).

prec

Gives the number of digits (i.e., precision) to include after . (use * to fetch from values).

typecode

A character from Table 8.

Both *width* and *prec* can be coded as a * to force their values to be taken from the next item in the values to the right of the % operator when sizes are not known until runtime. Hint: %s generically converts any object type to its print representation string.

Table 8. % string formatting type codes

Code	Meaning	Code	Meaning
s	String (or any object, uses str())	X	x with uppercase
r	s, but uses repr(), not str()	e	Floating-point exponent
c	Character (int or str)	E	e with uppercase
d	Decimal (base 10 integer)	f	Floating-point decimal
i	Integer	F	f with uppercase
u	Same as d (obsolete)	g	Floating-point e or f
o	Octal (base 8 integer)	G	Floating-point E or F
x	Hex (base 16 integer)	%	Literal '%' (coded as %%)

String formatting method

The formatting *method* call works similar to the prior section's expression, but is invoked with normal method-call syntax on the format string object, which identifies substitution targets with {} syntax instead of %.

Substitution targets in the format string may name method-call arguments by position or keyword name; may further reference argument attributes, keys, and offsets; may accept default formatting or provide explicit type codes; and may nest target syntax to pull values from the arguments list:

```
>>> 'The knights who say {0}!'.format('Ni')
'The knights who say Ni!'
>>> '{0} {1}, {2:.0f} you'.format(1, 'spam', 4.0)
'1 spam, 4 you'
>>> '{n} named {x:s}'.format(n=1, x="spam")
'1 named spam'
>>> '{n:.0E} => [{x:<6s}]'.format(
                         **dict(n=100, x='spam'))
```

```
'1E+02 => [spam   ]'
>>> '{:f}, {:.2f}, {:+.{}f}'.format(
                            1/3.0, 1/3.0, 1/3.0, 4)
'0.333333, 0.33, +0.3333'
```

Most format method applications have equivalents in % expression usage patterns as shown in the preceding section (e.g., dictionary key and * value references), although the method allows some operations to be coded inside the format string itself:

```
>>> import sys    # Method vs expr: attr, key, index

>>> fmt = '{0.platform} {1[x]} {2[0]}'
>>> fmt.format(sys, dict(x='ham'), 'AB')
'win32 ham A'

>>> fmt = '%s %s %s'
>>> fmt % (sys.platform, dict(x='ham')['x'], 'AB'[0])
'win32 ham A'
```

As of Python 3.1 and 2.7, a , (comma) preceding an integer or floating-point designation in *typecode*, formally described in "Formatting method syntax", inserts thousands-separator commas, and a *typecode* of % formats a percentage (tools not present in the formatting expression itself, but straightforward to code as reusable functions):

```
>>> '{0:,d}'.format(1000000)
'1,000,000'
>>> '{0:13,.2f}'.format(1000000)
' 1,000,000.00'
>>> '{0:%} {1:,.2%}'.format(1.23, 1234)
'123.000000% 123,400.00%'
```

Also as of Python 3.1 and 2.7, field numbers are automatically numbered sequentially if omitted from the *fieldname* also described in "Formatting method syntax"—the following three have the same effect, although auto-numbered fields may be less readable if many fields are present:

```
>>> '{0}/{1}/{2}'.format('usr', 'home', 'bob')
'usr/home/bob'
>>> '{}/{}/{}'.format('usr', 'home', 'bob')    # Auto
```

```
'usr/home/bob'
>>> '%s/%s/%s' % ('usr', 'home', 'bob')        # Expr
'usr/home/bob'
```

A single object may also be formatted with the format(*object*, *formatspec*) built-in function (see "Built-in Functions"), which is employed by the string format method, and whose behavior may be implemented with the __format__ operator-overloading method in classes (see "Operator Overloading Methods").

Formatting method syntax

Substitution targets in strings used for format method calls take the following general form, all four parts of which are optional, and must appear without intervening spaces (used here for clarity):

{*fieldname component* !*conversionflag* :*formatspec*}

In this substitution target syntax:

fieldname
> An optional number or keyword identifying an argument, which may be omitted to use relative argument numbering in 2.7, 3.1, and later.

component
> A string of zero or more .*name* or [*index*] references used to fetch attributes and indexed values of the argument, which may be omitted to use the whole argument value.

conversionflag
> Introduced by a ! if present, which is followed by r, s, or a to call repr(), str(), or ascii() built-in functions on the value, respectively.

formatspec
> Introduced by a : if present, and consists of text that specifies how the value should be presented, including details such as field width, alignment, padding, decimal precision, and so on, and ending with an optional datatype code.

The nested *formatspec* component after the colon character has a syntax of its own, formally described as follows (brackets in this denote optional components and are not coded literally):

```
[[fill]align][sign][#][0][width][,][.prec][typecode]
```

In this *formatspec* nested syntax:

fill

Can be any fill character other than { or }.

align

May be <, >, =, or ^, for left alignment, right alignment, padding after a sign character, or centered alignment, respectively.

sign

May be +, -, or space.

, (comma)

Requests a comma for a thousands separator as of Python 3.1 and 2.7.

width and prec

Much as in the % expression, and the *formatspec* may also contain nested {} format strings having a *fieldname* only, to take values from the arguments list dynamically (much like the * in formatting expressions). A 0 preceding *width* enables sign-aware zero padding (similar to *fill*), and a # enables an alternative conversion (if available).

typecode

Largely the same as in % expressions and listed in Table 8, but the format method has an extra b type code used to give integers in binary format (much like using the bin built-in); has an extra % type code to format percentages as of Python 3.1 and 2.7; and uses only d for base-10 integers (i or u are not used).

Note that unlike the expression's generic %s, the method's s type code requires a *string* object argument; omit the type code to accept any type generically in the method.

Template string substitution

As of Python 2.4, another form of string substitution is provided as an alternative to the string formatting expression and method described in the prior sections. In full formatting, substitution is achieved with the % operator or str.format() method (all four of the following return '2: PR5E'):

```
'%(page)i: %(book)s' % {'page': 2, 'book': 'PR5E'}
'%(page)i: %(book)s' % dict(page=2, book='PR5E')

'{page}: {book}'.format(**dict(page=2, book='PR5E'))
'{page}: {book}'.format(page=2, book='PR5E')
```

For simpler substitution tasks, a Template class in string uses $ to indicate a substitution:

```
>>> import string
>>> t = string.Template('$page: $book')
>>> t.substitute({'page': 2, 'book': 'PR5E'})
'2: PR5E'
```

Substitution values can be provided as keyword arguments or dictionary keys:

```
>>> s = string.Template('$who likes $what')
>>> s.substitute(who='bob', what=3.14)
'bob likes 3.14'
>>> s.substitute(dict(who='bob', what='pie'))
'bob likes pie'
```

A safe_substitute method ignores missing keys rather than raising an exception:

```
>>> t = string.Template('$page: $book')
>>> t.safe_substitute({'page': 3})
'3: $book'
```

String methods

In addition to the format() method described earlier, string method calls provide higher-level text processing tools beyond string expressions. Table 9 lists available string method calls; in this table, S is any string object (technically, a 3.X str). String methods that modify text always return a new string and never modify the object in-place (strings are immutable).

For more details on methods in the table, see the functional area description sections ahead, or run a help(str.*method*) interactively. Hint: this list can vary across Python releases; to see yours, try:

```
sorted(x for x in dir(str) if not x.startswith('__'))
```

See also the re module in "The re Pattern-Matching Module" for pattern-based equivalents to some string type methods.

Table 9. Python 3.X string method calls

```
S.capitalize()
S.casefold() (as of Python 3.3)
S.center(width, [, fill])
S.count(sub[, start[, end]])
S.encode([encoding[, errors]])
S.endswith(suffix[, start[, end]])
S.expandtabs([tabsize])
S.find(sub[, start[, end]])
S.format(*args, **kwargs)
S.format_map(mapping) (as of Python 3.2)
S.index(sub[, start[, end]])
S.isalnum()
S.isalpha()
S.isdecimal()
S.isdigit()
S.isidentifier()
S.islower()
S.isnumeric()
S.isprintable()
```

```
S.isspace()
S.istitle()
S.isupper()
S.join(iterable)
S.ljust(width[, fill])
S.lower()
S.lstrip([chars])
S.maketrans(x[, y[, z]])
S.partition(sep)
S.replace(old, new[, count])
S.rfind(sub[, start[, end]])
S.rindex(sub[, start[, end]])
S.rjust(width[, fill])
S.rpartition(sep)
S.rsplit([sep[, maxsplit]])
S.rstrip([chars])
S.split([sep[, maxsplit]])
S.splitlines([keepends])
S.startswith(prefix[, start[, end]])
S.strip([chars])
S.swapcase()
S.title()
S.translate(map)
S.upper()
S.zfill(width)
```

byte and bytearray methods

Python 3.X bytes and bytearray string types have method sets
similar to that of the normal str type given in the preceding section, but do not overlap exactly due to differing roles. (str is
Unicode text, bytes is raw binary data, and bytearray is mutable.)
In the following, run in Python 3.3, set(dir(X)) - set(dir(Y))
computes attributes unique to X:

```
>>> set(dir(str)) - set(dir(bytes))
{'__rmod__', 'encode', 'isnumeric', 'format',
'isidentifier', 'isprintable', 'isdecimal',
'format_map', '__mod__', 'casefold'}

>>> set(dir(bytes)) - set(dir(str))
{'decode', 'fromhex'}

>>> set(dir(bytearray)) - set(dir(bytes))
{'extend', 'remove', 'insert', 'append', 'pop',
'__iadd__', 'reverse', 'clear', '__imul__',
'copy', '__setitem__', '__alloc__', '__delitem__'}
```

Of note:

- str does not support Unicode *decoding* (it is already-
  decoded text), but may be *encoded* to bytes.

- bytes and bytearray do not support Unicode *encoding*
  (they are raw bytes, including both media and already-
  encoded text), but may be *decoded* to str.

- bytes and bytearray do not support string *formatting* (implemented by str.format and the % operator's __mod__ and
  __rmod__).

- bytearray has extra mutable in-place methods and operators similar to list (e.g., append, +=).

See "byte and bytearray strings" for more on byte string operations. Also see "Unicode Strings" for more on string type models,
and "Built-in Functions" for more on construction calls.

The next few sections go into more detail on selected methods listed in Table 9, grouped by functional area. In all of the documented calls that return a string result, the result is a *new string* (because strings are immutable, they are never modified in-place.) Whitespace in this coverage means spaces, tabs, and end-of-line characters (everything in string.whitespace).

Searching methods

S.find(*sub* [, *start* [, *end*]])
> Returns offset of the first occurrence of string *sub* in S, between offsets *start* and *end* (which default to 0 and len(S), the entire string). Returns –1 if not found. Hint: also see the in membership operator (in Table 3), which may be used to test substring membership in a string.

S.rfind(*sub* [, *start* [, *end*]])
> Like find, but scans from the end (right to left).

S.index(*sub* [, *start* [, *end*]])
> Like find, but raises ValueError if not found instead of returning –1.

S.rindex(*sub* [, *start* [, *end*]])
> Like rfind, but raises ValueError if not found instead of returning –1.

S.count(*sub* [, *start* [, *end*]])
> Counts the number of nonoverlapping occurrences of *sub* in S, from offsets *start* to *end* (defaults: 0, len(S)).

`S.startswith(sub [, start [, end]])`

> True if string `S` starts with substring `sub`. `start` and `end` give optional begin and end points for matching `sub`.

`S.endswith(sub [, start [, end]])`

> True if string `S` ends with substring `sub`. `start` and `end` give optional begin and end points for matching `sub`.

Splitting and joining methods

`S.split([sep [, maxsplit]])`

> Returns a list of the words in the string `S`, using `sep` as the delimiter string. If `maxsplit` is given, at most `maxsplit` splits are done. If `sep` is not specified or is None, any whitespace string is a separator. `'a*b'.split('*')` yields `['a','b']`. Hint: use `list(S)` to convert a string to a list of characters (e.g., `['a','*','b']`).

`S.join(iterable)`

> Concatenates an iterable (e.g., list or tuple) of strings into a single string, with `S` added between each item. `S` can be '' (an empty string) to convert an iterable of characters to a string (`'*'.join(['a','b'])` yields `'a*b'`).

`S.replace(old, new [, count])`

> Returns a copy of string `S` with all occurrences of substring `old` replaced by `new`. If `count` is passed, the first `count` occurrences are replaced. This works like a combination of `x=S.split(old)` and `new.join(x)`.

`S.splitlines([keepends])`

> Splits string `S` on line breaks, returning lines list. The result does not retain line break characters unless `keepends` is true.

Formatting methods

`S.format(*args, **kwargs)`, `S.format_map(mapping)`

> See section "String formatting". In Python 3.2 and later, `S.format_map(M)` is like `S.format(**M)`, but `M` is not copied.

`S.capitalize()`

> Capitalizes the first character of string S, and lowercases its other characters.

`S.expandtabs([`*`tabsize`*`])`

> Replaces tabs in string S with *tabsize* spaces (default is 8).

`S.strip([`*`chars`*`])`

> Removes leading and trailing whitespace from string S (or characters in *chars* if passed).

`S.lstrip([`*`chars`*`])`

> Removes leading whitespace from string S (or characters in *chars* if passed).

`S.rstrip([`*`chars`*`])`

> Removes trailing whitespace from string S (or characters in *chars* if passed).

`S.swapcase()`

> Converts all lowercase letters to uppercase, and vice versa.

`S.upper()`

> Converts all letters to uppercase.

`S.lower()`

> Converts all letters to lowercase.

`S.casefold()`

> In Python 3.3 and later, returns a version of S suitable for caseless comparisons; like `S.lower()`, but also intelligently lowercases some Unicode characters.

`S.ljust(`*`width`*` [, `*`fill`*`])`

> Left-justifies string S in a field of the given *width*; pads on right with character *fill* (which defaults to a space). The string formatting expression and method can achieve similar effects.

`S.rjust(`*`width`*` [, `*`fill`*`])`

> Right-justifies string S in a field of the given *width*; pads on left with character *fill* (which defaults to a space). The

string formatting expression and method can achieve similar effects.

`S.center(width [, fill])`

Centers string S in a field of the given *width*; pads on left and right with character *fill* (which defaults to a space). String formatting can achieve similar effects.

`S.zfill(width)`

Pads string S on left with zero digits to produce a string result of the desired *width* (can also achieve with string formatting).

`S.translate(table [, deletechars])`

Deletes all characters from string S that are in *deletechars* (if present), and then translates the characters using *table*, a 256-character string giving the translation for each character value indexed by its ordinal.

`S.title()`

Returns a title-cased version of the string: words start with uppercase characters; all remaining cased characters are lowercase.

Content test methods

`S.is*()`

The `is*()` Boolean tests work on strings of any length. They test the content of strings for various categories (and always return False for an empty).

The original string module

Starting in Python 2.0, most of the string-processing functions previously available in the standard `string` module became available as methods of string objects. If X references a string object, a `string` module function call such as:

```
import string
res = string.replace(X, 'span', 'spam')
```

is usually equivalent in Python 2.0 and later to a string method call such as:

```
res = X.replace('span', 'spam')
```

But the string method call form is preferred and quicker, and string methods require no module imports. Note that the `string.join(iterable, delim)` operation becomes a method of the delimiter string `delim.join(iterable)`. All these functions are removed from the `string` module in Python 3.X: use the equivalent string object methods instead. See "The string Module" for this module's remaining content.

Unicode Strings

All text is Unicode text, including text encoded with one character per byte (8 bits) in the ASCII scheme. Python supports richer character sets and encoding schemes with *Unicode*—strings which may use multiple bytes to represent characters in memory, and which translate text to and from various encodings on files. This support differs in Python lines. Python 3.X treats all text as Unicode and represents binary data separately, while Python 2.X distinguishes 8-bit text (and data) from possibly wider Unicode text:

In Python 3.X

> The normal `str` type and `'ccc'` literal represents all text, both 8-bit and richer Unicode. `str` is an immutable sequence of *characters*—decoded Unicode code points (ordinal identifiers) in memory.

> A separate `bytes` type and `b'ccc'` literal represents binary data byte values, including media and encoded Unicode text. `bytes` is an immutable sequence of small *integers* (8-bit byte values), but supports most `str` operations, and prints content as ASCII characters when possible. An additional `bytearray` type is a mutable variant of `bytes`, with extra list-like methods for in-place changes.

Also in 3.X, normal *files* created by open() imply str and bytes objects for content in text and binary mode, respectively. In text mode, files automatically encode on output and decode on input.

As of Python 3.3, 2.X's u'ccc' Unicode literal form is also available for backward compatibility with 2.X code (it creates a 3.X str).

In Python 2.X

The normal str type and 'ccc' literal represents the byte values of both 8-bit oriented text and binary data, and a separate unicode type and u'ccc' literal represents the code points of possibly wider Unicode text. Both string types are immutable sequences, and have nearly identical operations.

Also in 2.X, normal *files* created by open() are byte-oriented, and a codecs.open() supports reading and writing files containing Unicode text with encoding and decoding on transfers.

As of Python 2.6, 3.X's b'ccc' bytes literal is also available for forward compatibility with 3.X code (it creates a 2.X str), and 3.X's mutable bytearray is present though less type specific.

Unicode support in Python 3.X

Python 3.X allows non-ASCII characters to be coded in strings with hex (\x) and both 16- and 32-bit Unicode (\u, \U) escapes. In addition, chr() supports Unicode character codes:

```
>>> 'A\xE4B'
'AäB'
>>> 'A\u00E4B'
'AäB'
>>> 'A\U000000E4B'
'AäB'
>>> chr(0xe4)
'ä'
```

Normal strings may be encoded into raw bytes and raw bytes may be decoded into normal strings, using either default or explicit encodings (and optional error policy: see str() in "Built-in Functions"):

```
>>> 'A\xE4B'.encode('latin-1')
b'A\xe4B'
>>> 'A\xE4B'.encode()
b'A\xc3\xa4B'
>>> 'A\xE4B'.encode('utf-8')
b'A\xc3\xa4B'

>>> b'A\xC3\xA4B'.decode('utf-8')
'AäB'
```

File objects also automatically encode on output and decode on input in text mode (but not in binary mode), and accept an encoding name to override the default encoding (see open() in "Built-in Functions"):

```
>>> S = 'A\xE4B'
>>> open('uni.txt', 'w', encoding='utf-8').write(S)
3
>>> open('uni.txt', 'rb').read()
b'A\xc3\xa4B'
>>>
>>> open('uni.txt', 'r', encoding='utf-8').read()
'AäB'
```

As of release 3.3, Python 3.X also supports 2.X's u'ccc' Unicode literal form for backward compatibility, but it is a synonym for 'ccc', and creates a normal 3.X str string.

In both 3.X and 2.X, you may also embed Unicode content in program source files directly: use a line of the following form as line 1 or 2 of your file, if needed to override Python's UTF-8 default:

```
# -*- coding: latin-1 -*-
```

byte and bytearray strings

Python 3.X bytes and bytearray string objects represent 8-bit binary data (including encoded Unicode text); are printed as ASCII text when possible; and support most normal str string operations including methods and sequence operations (but not string formatting):

```
>>> B = b'spam'
>>> B
b'spam'
>>> B[0]                # Sequence ops
115
>>> B + b'abc'
b'spamabc'
>>> B.split(b'a')       # Methods
[b'sp', b'm']
>>> list(B)             # Sequence of int
[115, 112, 97, 109]
```

bytearray additionally supports list-like mutable operations:

```
>>> BA = bytearray(b'spam')
>>> BA
bytearray(b'spam')
>>> BA[0]
115
>>> BA + b'abc'
bytearray(b'spamabc')
>>> BA[0] = 116         # Mutability
>>> BA.append(115)      # List methods
>>> BA
bytearray(b'tpams')
```

Formally, both bytes and bytearray support *sequence operations* (see Table 3), as well as type-specific *methods* described earlier in "byte and bytearray methods". bytearray additionally supports *mutable sequence operations* (see Table 4). See also type constructor calls in "Built-in Functions".

Python 2.6 and 2.7 have bytearray but not bytes—3.X's b'ccc' is supported for forward compatibility, but is simply a synonym for 'ccc', and creates a normal 2.X str string.

Unicode support in Python 2.X

In Python 2.X, Unicode strings are written as u'ccc', which creates a unicode type object. (In Python 3.X, the normal string type and literal are used for Unicode.) Arbitrary Unicode characters can be written using a special escape sequence, \uHHHH, where HHHH is a four-digit hexadecimal number from 0000 to FFFF. The traditional \xHH escape sequence can also be used, and octal escapes can be used for characters up to +01FF, which is represented by \777.

unicode supports both string methods and *sequence operations* (see Table 3). Normal and Unicode string objects can be mixed in Python 2.X; combining 8-bit and Unicode strings always coerces to Unicode, using the default ASCII encoding (e.g., the result of 'a' + u'bc' is u'abc'). Mixed-type operations assume the 8-bit string contains 7-bit U.S. ASCII data (and raise an error for non-ASCII characters). The built-in str() and unicode() functions can be used to convert between normal and Unicode strings, and the encode() and decode() string methods apply and undo Unicode encodings.

Available related modules and built-in functions include codecs.open(), whose files perform Unicode encoding translations on data transfers, much like 3.X's built-in open() function files.

Lists

Lists are *mutable* (changeable) *sequences* of object references accessed by *offset* (position).

Literals and creation

List literals are written as a comma-separated series of values enclosed in square brackets, and various operations construct lists dynamically:

```
[]
```
An empty list.

```
[0, 1, 2, 3]
```
A four-item list: indexes 0 through 3.

```
L = ['spam', [42, 3.1415], 1.23, {}]
```
Nested sublists: L[1][0] fetches 42.

```
L = list('spam')
```
Creates a list of all items in any iterable, by calling the type constructor function.

```
L = [x ** 2 for x in range(9)]
```
Creates a list by collecting expression results during iteration (list comprehension).

Operations

Operations include all *sequence operations* (see Table 3), plus all *mutable sequence operations* (see Table 4), plus the following list-specific *methods*, in all of which L stands for any list object:

```
L.append(X)
```
Inserts the single object X at the end of L, changing the list in-place.

```
L.extend(I)
```
Inserts each item in any iterable I at the end of L in-place (like an in-place +). Similar to L[len(L):] = I. Hint: use L[:0] = I to prepend all items in I.

```
L.sort(key=None, reverse=False)
```
Sorts L in-place, in ascending order by default. If passed, key specifies a function of one argument that is used to extract or compute a comparison value from each list element. If reverse is passed and true, the list elements are sorted as if each comparison were reversed. For example: L.sort(key=str.lower, reverse=True). See also sorted() in "Built-in Functions".

`L.reverse()`

Reverses items in *L* in-place. See also `reversed()` in "Built-in Functions".

`L.index(X [, i [, j]])`

Returns the index of the first occurrence of object *X* in *L*; raises an exception if not found. This is a search method. If *i* and possibly *j* are passed, it returns the smallest k such that `L[k] == X` and `i <= k < j`, where *j* defaults to `len(L)`.

`L.insert(i, X)`

Inserts single object *X* into *L* at offset *i* (like `L[i:i]` = `[X]`, for positive or negative *i*). Hint: use `L[i:i]` = `I` to insert all items in any iterable *I* at offset *i*.

`L.count(X)`

Returns the number of occurrences of *X* in *L*.

`L.remove(X)`

Deletes the first occurrence of object *X* from *L*; raises an exception if not found. Same as `del L[L.index(X)]`.

`L.pop([i])`

Deletes and returns the last (or offset *i*) item in *L*. Useful with `append()` to implement stacks. Same as `x=L[i]`; `del L[i]`; `return x`, where *i* defaults to -1, the last item.

`L.clear()`

Removes all items from *L*. Available in 3.X (only), as of 3.3.

`L.copy()`

Make a top-level (shallow) copy of *L*. Available in 3.X (only), as of 3.3

NOTE

In Python 2.X, the list sort method signature is:
```
L.sort(cmp=None, key=None, reverse=False)
```

where cmp is a two-argument comparison function, which returns a value less than, equal to, or greater than zero to denote a less, equal, and greater result. The comparison function is removed in 3.X because it was typically used to map sort values and reverse sort order—use cases supported by the remaining two arguments.

List comprehension expressions

A list literal enclosed in square brackets ([...]) can be a simple list of expressions or a list comprehension expression of the following form:

```
[expr for target1 in iterable1 [if condition1]
      for target2 in iterable2 [if condition2] ...
      for targetN in iterableN [if conditionN] ]
```

List comprehensions construct result lists: they collect all values of expression *expr*, for each iteration of all nested for loops, for which each optional *condition* is true. The second through N^{th} for loops and all if parts are optional, and *expr* and each *condition* can use variables assigned by nested for loops. Names bound (assigned) inside a list comprehension are created in the scope enclosing the comprehension expression in 2.X, but are localized to the comprehension in 3.X. Comprehensions may be nested arbitrarily.

Comprehensions are similar to the map() built-in function (in 3.X only, map() requires list() to force results generation for display, because it both iterates and is iterable itself; in 2.X map() returns a list):

```
>>> [ord(x) for x in 'spam']
[115, 112, 97, 109]
>>> list(map(ord, 'spam'))        # Use list() in 3.X
[115, 112, 97, 109]
```

However, comprehensions can often avoid creating a temporary helper function:

```
>>> [x ** 2 for x in range(5)]
[0, 1, 4, 9, 16]
>>> list(map((lambda x: x ** 2), range(5)))
[0, 1, 4, 9, 16]
```

Comprehensions with conditions are similar to filter() (also an iterable in 3.X only):

```
>>> [x for x in range(5) if x % 2 == 0]
[0, 2, 4]
>>> list(filter((lambda x: x % 2 == 0), range(5)))
[0, 2, 4]
```

Comprehensions with nested for loops are similar to the normal for statement:

```
>>> [x + y for x in range(3) for y in [10, 20, 30]]
[10, 20, 30, 11, 21, 31, 12, 22, 32]

>>> res = []
>>> for x in range(3):
...     for y in [10, 20, 30]:
...         res.append(x + y)
...
>>> res
[10, 20, 30, 11, 21, 31, 12, 22, 32]
```

The iteration protocol

The *iteration protocol* defines a set of objects and methods used by all *iteration contexts*—including comprehensions, for loop statements, and built-in functions such as map() and filter()—to automatically step through items in collections or results produced on demand. Iteration works as follows:

- Iteration contexts operate on an *iterable*—an object with an __iter__() method.

- When called, the iterable's __iter__() method returns an *iterator*—an object with a __next__() method (possibly the same object).

- When called, the iterator's __next__() method returns the next item in the iteration or raises a StopIteration exception to end the iteration.

In addition, the iter(X) built-in function invokes an iterable's X.__iter__() method, and the next(I) built-in function calls an iterator's I.__next__() method, both to simplify manual iteration loops and as a portability layer. Some tools, such as the map() built-in and the *generator expression*, are both iteration context (for their subject) and iterable object (for their results); see prior and next sections.

Classes can provide an __iter__() method to intercept the iter(X) built-in operation; if defined, its result has a __next__() method used to step through results in iteration contexts. If no __iter__() is defined, the __getitem__() indexing method is used as a fallback to iterate until IndexError.

In *Python 2.X*, the I.__next__() iterator objects' method is named I.next(), but iteration works the same otherwise. The next(I) built-in function calls the I.next() method in 2.6 and 2.7 instead of I.__next__(), making it useful for both 3.X compatibility in 2.X, and 2.X compatibility in 3.X.

Generator expressions

As of Python 2.4, generator expressions achieve effects similar to list comprehensions, without generating a physical list to hold all results. Generator expressions define a set of results, but do not materialize the entire list, to save memory; instead, they create a *generator object* that will return elements one by one in iteration contexts by automatically supporting the *iteration protocol* of the prior section. For example:

```
ords = (ord(x) for x in aString if x not in skipStr)
for o in ords:
    ...
```

Generator expressions are comprehensions coded inside parentheses rather than square brackets, but otherwise support all list comprehension syntax. The parentheses used for a function with a single argument suffice when creating an iterable to be passed to a function:

```
sum(ord(x) for x in aString)
```

Generator expression loop variables (e.g., x, in the prior example) are not accessible outside the generator expression in either Python 2.X or 3.X. In 2.X, list comprehensions leave the loop variable assigned to its last value, but all other comprehensions localize the variable to the expression; in Python 3.X, loop variables are localized to the expression in all comprehension forms.

To step through results outside iteration contexts such as for loops, use either the iteration protocol's `I.__next__()` method in 3.X, its `I.next()` method in Python 2.X, or the `next(I)` built-in function in either Python 2.X or 3.X, which calls the appropriate method portably. When required, use the `list()` call to produce all (remaining) results all at once (because generators are their own iterators, calling their `__iter__()` is harmless but not required):

```
>>> squares = (x ** 2 for x in range(5))
>>> squares
<generator object <genexpr> at 0x027C1AF8>

>>> iter(squares) is squares    # __iter__() optional
True
>>> squares.__next__()          # Method (.next in 2.X)
0
>>> next(squares)               # Built-in (3.X, 2.6+)
1
>>> list(squares)               # Till StopIteration
[4, 9, 16]
```

See "The iteration protocol" for more on the mechanism used by generator expressions, and "The yield Statement" for the related *generator function*, which also creates a generator object.

Other comprehension expressions

See also dictionary and set comprehensions elsewhere in this book (sections "Dictionaries" and "Sets"). These are similar expressions that produce dictionaries and sets all at once; they support syntax identical to list comprehensions and generator expressions, but are coded within {}, and dictionary comprehensions begin with a *key*:*value* expression pair:

```
>>> [x * x for x in range(10)]        # List comp
[0, 1, 4, 9, 16, 25, 36, 49, 64, 81]

>>> (x * x for x in range(10))        # Generator expr
<generator object <genexpr> at 0x009E7328>

>>> {x * x for x in range(10)}        # Set: 3.X, 2.7
{0, 1, 4, 81, 64, 9, 16, 49, 25, 36}

>>> {x: x * x for x in range(10)}     # Dict: 3.X, 2.7
{0: 0, 1: 1, 2: 4, 3: 9, 4: 16, 5: 25, 6: 36, 7: 49,
8: 64, 9: 81}
```

Dictionaries

Dictionaries are *mutable* (changeable) *mappings* of object references accessed by *key* (not position). They are unordered tables that map keys to values, implemented internally as dynamically expandable hash tables. Dictionaries differ substantially in Python 3.X:

- In *Python 2.X*, the keys()/values()/items() methods return lists; there is a has_key() lookup method; there are distinct iterable methods iterkeys()/itervalues()/iteritems(); and dictionaries may be compared directly. As of Python 2.7, 3.X's dictionary comprehensions are available as a back-port, and 3.X-style views are supported with methods viewkeys()/viewvalues()/viewitems().

- In *Python 3.X*, the keys()/values()/items() methods return iterable *view* objects instead of lists; has_key() is removed in favor of in expressions; Python 2.X iterable methods are removed in favor of *view* object iteration; dictionaries cannot be compared directly, but their sorted(*D*.items()) can; and there is a new dictionary comprehension expression.

- Python 3.X *view* objects produce results on demand, retain the original order in the dictionary, reflect future dictionary changes, and may support *set* operations. Key views are always set-like, value views never are, and item views are if all their items are unique and hashable (immutable). See "Sets" for set expressions that may be applied to some views. Pass views to the list() call to force generation of all their results at once (e.g., for display, or to apply the list's *L*.sort()).

Literals and creation

Dictionary literals are written as comma-separated series of *key*:*value* pairs inside curly braces, the dict() built-in supports other creation patterns, and dictionary comprehensions employ iteration in Python 3.X and 2.7. Assigning to new keys generates new entries.

Any *immutable* object can be a dictionary key (e.g., string, number, tuple), and class instances can be keys if they inherit hashing protocol methods (see __hash__ in "Operator Overloading Methods"). Tuple keys support compound values (e.g., adict[(M,D,Y)], with parentheses optional):

{}
    An empty dictionary (not a set).

{'spam': 2, 'eggs': 3}
    A two-item dictionary: keys 'spam' and 'eggs', values 2 and 3.

D = {'info': {42: 1, type(''): 2}, 'spam': []}
    Nested dictionaries: D['info'][42] fetches 1.

```
D = dict(name='Bob', age=45, job=('mgr', 'dev'))
```
Creates a dictionary by passing keyword arguments to the type constructor.

```
D = dict(zip('abc', [1, 2, 3]))
```
Creates a dictionary by passing key/value tuple pairs to the type constructor.

```
D = dict([['a', 1], ['b', 2], ['c', 3]])
```
Same effect as prior line: accepts any iterable of keys and values.

```
D = {c.upper(): ord(c) for c in 'spam'}
```
Dictionary comprehension expression (in Python 3.X and 2.7). See "List comprehension expressions" for full syntax.

Operations

Operations comprise all *mapping operations* (see Table 5), plus the following dictionary-specific *methods*, in all of which *D* stands for any dictionary object:

`D.keys()`
> All keys in *D*. In Python 2.X, this returns a list. In Python 3.X, it returns an iterable view object described earlier. `for K in D` also supports keys iteration implicitly.

`D.values()`
> All stored values in *D*. In Python 2.X, this returns a list. In Python 3.X, it returns an iterable view object described earlier.

`D.items()`
> Tuple pairs (*key, value*), one for each entry in *D*. In Python 2.X, this returns a list. In Python 3.X, it returns an iterable view object described earlier.

`D.clear()`
> Removes all items from *D*.

`D.copy()`
> Returns a shallow (top-level) copy of *D*.

`D.update(D2)`

> Merges all of *D2*'s entries into *D*, in-place, similar to `for (k, v) in D2.items(): D[k] = v`. In Python 2.4 and later, also accepts an iterable of key/value pairs, as well as keyword arguments (e.g., `D.update(k1=v1, k2=v2)`).

`D.get(K [, default])`

> Similar to *D[K]* for key *K*, but returns *default* (or None if no *default*) instead of raising an exception when *K* is not found in *D*.

`D.setdefault(K, [, default])`

> Same as `D.get(K, default)`, but also assigns key *K* to *default* if it is not found in *D*.

`D.popitem()`

> Removes and returns an arbitrary *(key, value)* tuple pair.

`D.pop(K [, default])`

> If key *K* in *D*, returns *D[K]* and removes *K*; else, returns *default* if given, or raises KeyError if no default.

`dict.fromkeys(I [, value])`

> Creates a new dictionary with keys from iterable *I* and values each set to *value* (default None). Callable on an instance *D* or type name dict.

The following methods are available in *Python 2.X* only:

`D.has_key(K)`

> Returns True if *D* has a key *K*, or False otherwise. In Python 2.X only, this method is equivalent to *K* in *D*, but is not generally recommended, as it is removed in Python 3.X.

`D.iteritems(), D.iterkeys(), D.itervalues()`

> Return iterables over key/value pairs, keys only, or values only. In Python 3.X, these are removed because `items()`, `keys()`, and `values()` return iterable view objects.

`D.viewitems()`, `D.viewkeys()`, `D.viewvalues()`

Available as of 2.7, these return iterable view objects over key/value pairs, keys only, or values only, to emulate the view objects returned by 3.X's `items()`, `keys()`, and `values()`.

The following operations are described in Table 5, but relate to preceding methods:

`K in D`

Returns `True` if `D` has key `K`, or `False` otherwise. Replaces `has_key()` in Python 3.X.

`for K in D`

Iterates over keys `K` in `D` (all iteration contexts). Dictionary supports direct iteration: `for K in D` is similar to `for K in D.keys()`. The former uses the dictionary object's keys iterator. In Python 2.X, `keys()` returns a new list that incurs a slight overhead. In Python 3.X, `keys()` returns an iterable view object instead of a physically stored list, making both forms equivalent.

Tuples

Tuples are *immutable* (unchangeable) *sequences* of object references accessed by *offset* (position).

Literals and creation

Tuple literals are written as comma-separated series of values enclosed in parentheses. The enclosing parentheses can sometimes be omitted (e.g., in `for` loop headers and `=` assignments):

`()`

An empty tuple.

`(0,)`

A one-item tuple (not a simple expression).

`(0, 1, 2, 3)`

A four-item tuple.

```
0, 1, 2, 3
```
Another four-item tuple (same as prior line); not valid where comma or parentheses are otherwise significant (e.g., function arguments, 2.X prints).

```
T = ('spam', (42, 'eggs'))
```
Nested tuples: T[1][1] fetches 'eggs'.

```
T = tuple('spam')
```
Creates a tuple of all items in any iterable, by calling the type constructor function.

Operations

All *sequence operations* (see Table 3), plus the following tuple-specific *methods* in Python 2.6, 3.0, and later in both lines:

`T.index(X [, i [, j]])`

Returns the index of the first occurrence of object X in tuple T; raises an exception if not found. This is a search method. If i and possibly j are passed, it returns the smallest k such that $T[k] == X$ and $i <= k < j$, where j defaults to len(T).

`T.count(X)`

Returns the number of occurrences of X in tuple T.

Files

The built-in open() function creates a *file object*, the most common interface to external files. File objects export the data transfer methods in the following sections, where file content is represented as Python strings. This is a partial list: see Python manuals for lesser-used calls and attributes.

In Python 2.X only, the name file() can be used as a synonym for open() when creating a file object, but open() is the generally recommended spelling. In Python 3.X, file() is no longer available. (The io module's classes are used for file customization.)

See the open() function in "Built-in Functions" for more complete file-creation details. See also "Unicode Strings" for the distinction between text and binary files and their corresponding implied string type differences for content in Python 3.X.

Related file-like tools covered later in this book: see the dbm, shelve, and pickle modules in "Object Persistence Modules"; the os module file descriptor-based file functions and the os.path directory path tools in "The os System Module"; JSON file storage in "The json Module"; and SQL database usage in "Python SQL Database API".

See also Python's manuals for *socketobj*.makefile() to convert a socket to a file-like object, and io.StringIO(*str*) and io.BytesIO(*bytes*) (StringIO.StringIO(*str*) in Python 2.X) to convert a string to a file-like object, compatible with APIs that expect the file object interface defined here.

Input files

infile = open(*filename*, 'r')
> Creates input file object, connected to the named external file. *filename* is normally a string (e.g., 'data.txt'), and maps to the current working directory unless it includes a directory path prefix (e.g., r'c:\dir\data.txt'). Argument two gives file *mode*: 'r' reads text, 'rb' reads binary with no line-break translation. Mode is optional and defaults to 'r'. Python 3.X's open() also accepts an optional Unicode encoding name in text mode; 2.X's codecs.open() has similar tools.

infile.read()
> Reads entire file, returning its contents as a single string. In text mode ('r'), line-ends are translated to '\n' by default. In binary mode ('rb'), the result string can contain nonprintable characters (e.g., '\0'). In Python 3.X, text mode *decodes* Unicode text into a str string, and binary mode returns unaltered content in a bytes string.

infile.read(*N*)
> Reads at most *N* more bytes (1 or more); empty at end-of-file.

infile.readline()

> Reads next line (through end-of-line marker); empty at end-of-file.

infile.readlines()

> Reads entire file into a list of line strings. See also the file object's line iterator alternative, discussed in the next list item.

for *line* in *infile*

> Uses the *line iterator* of file object *infile* to step through lines in the file automatically. Available in all iteration contexts, including for loops, map(), and comprehensions (e.g., [line.rstrip() for line in open('*filename*')]). The iteration for *line* in *infile* has an effect similar to for *line* in *infile*.readlines(), but the line iterator version fetches lines on demand instead of loading the entire file into memory, and so is more space-efficient.

Output files

outfile = open(*filename*, 'w')

> Creates output file object, connected to external file named by *filename* (defined in the preceding section). Mode 'w' writes text, 'wb' writes binary data with no line-break translation. Python 3.X's open() also accepts an optional Unicode encoding name in text mode; 2.X's codecs.open() has similar tools.

outfile.write(*S*)

> Writes all content in string *S* onto file, with no formatting applied. In text mode, '\n' is translated to the platform-specific line-end marker sequence by default. In binary mode, the string can contain nonprintable bytes (e.g., use 'a\0b\0c' to write a string of five bytes, two of which are binary zero). In Python 3.X, text mode requires str Unicode strings and *encodes* them when written, and binary mode expects and writes bytes strings unaltered.

---

outfile.writelines(*I*)

Writes all strings in iterable *I* onto file, not adding any line-end characters automatically.

Any files

file.close()

Manual close to free resources (although CPython currently auto-closes files if still open when they are garbage collected). See also the file object's context manager in "File context managers".

file.tell()

Returns the file's current position.

file.seek(*offset* [, *whence*])

Sets the current file position to *offset* for random access. *whence* can be 0 (offset from front), 1 (offset +/− from current position), or 2 (offset from end). *whence* defaults to 0.

file.isatty()

Returns True if the file is connected to a tty-like (interactive) device, else False (may return 1 or 0 in older Python versions).

file.flush()

Flushes the file's stdio buffer. Useful for buffered pipes, if another process (or human) is reading. Also useful for files created and read in the same process.

file.truncate([*size*])

Truncates file to, at most, *size* bytes (or current position if no size is passed). Not available on all platforms.

file.fileno()

Gets file number (file descriptor integer) for file. This roughly converts file objects to file descriptors that can be passed to tools in the os module. Hint: use os.fdopen() or 3.X's open() to convert a file descriptor to a file object.

Other file attributes (some read-only)

file.closed
>   True if file has been closed

file.mode
>   Mode string (e.g., 'r') passed to open() function

file.name
>   String name of corresponding external file

File context managers

In standard Python (CPython), file objects normally close themselves when garbage collected if still open. Because of this, temporary files (e.g., open('name').read()) suffice and need not be closed explicitly, as the file object is immediately reclaimed and closed. Other Python implementations (e.g., Jython), however, may collect and close files less deterministically.

To guarantee closes after a block of code exits, regardless of whether the block raises an exception, use the try/finally statement and manual closes:

```
myfile = open(r'C:\misc\script', 'w')
try:
    ...use myfile...
finally:
    myfile.close()
```

Or use the with/as statement available in Python 3.X and 2.X (as of 2.6 and 3.0):

```
with open(r'C:\misc\script', 'w') as myfile:
    ...use myfile...
```

The first of these inserts a close call as a termination-time action. The latter employs file object *context managers*, which guarantee that a file is automatically closed when the enclosed code block exits. See the try and with statements in "Statements and Syntax" for further details.

File usage notes

- Some file-open modes (e.g., `'r+'`) allow a file to be both input and output, and others (e.g., `'rb'`) specify binary-mode transfer to suppress line-end marker conversions (and Unicode encodings in Python 3.X). See `open()` in "Built-in Functions".

- File-transfer operations occur at the current file position, but `seek()` method calls reposition the file for random access.

- File transfers can be made *unbuffered*: see `open()` arguments in "Built-in Functions", and the `-u` command-line flag in "Python Command Options".

- Python 2.X also includes an `xreadlines()` file object method, which works the same as the file object's automatic line iterator, and has been removed in Python 3.X due to its redundancy.

Sets

Sets are *mutable* (changeable) and unordered collections of *unique and immutable* objects. Sets support mathematical set operations such as union and intersection. They are not sequences (they are unordered), and not mappings (they do not map values to keys), but support iteration, and function much like value-less (or keys-only) dictionaries.

Literals and creation

In Python 2.X and 3.X, sets may be created by calling the `set()` built-in function, passing it an iterable whose items become members of the resulting set. In Python 3.X and 2.7, sets may also be created by `{...}` set literal and set comprehension expression syntax, although `set()` is still used to make an empty set (`{}` is the empty dictionary), and to build sets from existing objects.

Sets are mutable, but items in a set must be immutable; the
frozenset() built-in creates an immutable set, which can be nested within another set:

```
set()
```
> An empty set ({} is an empty dictionary).

```
S = set('spam')
```
> A four-item set: values 's', 'p', 'a', 'm' (accepts any itera-
> ble).

```
S = {'s', 'p', 'a', 'm'}
```
> A four-item set, same as prior line (in Python 3.X and 2.7).

```
S = {ord(c) for c in 'spam'}
```
> Sets comprehension expression (in Python 3.X and 2.7); see
> "List comprehension expressions" for full syntax.

```
S = frozenset(range(-5, 5))
```
> A frozen (immutable) set of 10 integers, -5...4.

Operations

The following documents the most prominent set operations,
where *S*, *S1*, and *S2* are any set. Most expression operators require
two sets, but their method-based equivalents accept any *itera-
ble*, denoted by *other* in the following (e.g., {1, 2} | [2, 3] fails,
but {1, 2}.union([2, 3]) works). This list is representative but
not complete; see Python's Library Reference for an exhaustive
list of set expressions and methods available:

x in S
> Membership: returns True if set *S* contains *x*.

S1 - *S2*, *S1*.difference(*other*)
> Difference: new set containing items in *S1* that are not in *S2*
> (or *other*).

S1 | *S2*, *S1*.union(*other*)
> Union: new set containing items in either *S1* or *S2* (or
> *other*) with no duplicates.

S1 & S2, *S1*.intersection(*other*)

> Intersection: new set containing items in both *S1* and *S2* (or *other*).

S1 <= S2, *S1*.issubset(*other*)

> Subset: tests whether every element in *S1* is also in *S2* (or *other*).

S1 >= S2, *S1*.issuperset(*other*)

> Superset: tests whether every element in *S2* (or *other*) is also in *S1*.

S1 < S2, *S1 > S2*

> True subset and superset: also tests that *S1* and *S2* are not the same.

S1 ^ S2, *S1*.symmetric_difference(*other*)

> Symmetric difference: new set with elements in either *S1* or *S2* (or *other*) but not both.

S1 |= S2, *S1*.update(*other*)

> Updates (not for frozen sets): adds items in *S2* (or *other*) to *S1*.

S.add(*x*), *S*.remove(*x*), *S*.discard(*x*), *S*.pop(), *S*.clear()

> Updates (not for frozen sets): adds an item, removes an item by value, removes an item if present, removes and returns an arbitrary item, removes all items.

len(*S*)

> Length: numbers items in set.

for *x* in *S*

> Iteration: all iteration contexts.

S.copy()

> Makes a top-level (shallow) copy of *S*; same as set(*S*).

Other Types and Conversions

Python's core built-in types also include *Booleans*—described next; None—a false placeholder object; NotImplemented—used by operator overloading methods; Ellipsis—created by the ... literal in 3.X; *types*—accessed with the type() built-in function, and always classes in Python 3.X; and *program-unit types*—including functions, modules, and classes (all runtime and first-class objects in Python).

Boolean

The Boolean type, named bool, provides two predefined constants added to the built-in scope, named True and False (available since version 2.3). For most purposes, these constants can be treated as though they were preassigned to integers 1 and 0, respectively (e.g., True + 3 yields 4). However, the bool type is a subclass of the integer type int, and customizes it to print instances differently. (True prints as "True", not "1", and may be used as a built-in mnemonic name in logical tests.)

Type Conversions

Tables 10 and 11 list built-in tools for converting from one type to another. All of these make *new* objects (they are not in-place converters). Python 2.X also supports long(S) to-long and `X` to-string converters, both removed in Python 3.X. See also "Numbers" and "String formatting" for some of the tools listed in these tables.

Table 10. Sequence converters

Converter	Converts from	Converts to
list(X), [n for n in X][a]	String, tuple, any iterable	List
tuple(X)	String, list, any iterable	Tuple
''.join(X)	Iterable of strings	String

[a] The list comprehension form may (or may not) be slower than list(), and may not be best practice in this specific conversion context. In Python 2.X only, map(None, X) has the same effect as list(X) in this context, although this form of map() is removed in Python 3.X.

Table 11. String/object converters

Converter	Converts from	Converts to
eval(S)	String	Any object having expression syntax
int(S [, base]),[a] float(S)	String or number	Integer, float
repr(X), str(X)	Any Python object	String (repr is as-code, str is user-friendly)
F%X, F.format(X), format(X, [F])	Objects with format codes	String
hex(X), oct(X), bin(X), str(X)	Integer types	Hexadecimal, octal, binary, decimal digit strings
ord(C), chr(I)	Character, integer code	Integer code, character

[a] In version 2.2 and later, converter functions (e.g., int(), float(), str()) also serve as class constructors and can be subclassed. In Python 3.X, all types are classes, and all classes are instances of the type class.

Statements and Syntax

This section describes the rules for syntax and variable names.

Syntax Rules

The following are the general rules for writing Python programs:

Control flow

Statements execute sequentially, one after another, unless control-flow statements are used to branch elsewhere in code (e.g., if, while, for, raise, calls, etc.).

Blocks

A nested block is delimited by indenting all of its statements by the same amount, with any number of spaces or tabs used consistently. A nested block can also appear on the same line as its statement header (following the header's : character), if it consists of simple (noncompound) statements only.

As a rule of thumb, a given block should use all tabs *or* all spaces for indentation. Combinations of the two are formally analyzed by two rules: (*1*) a tab counts for enough spaces to move the column number to the next multiple of 8; and (*2*) additional inconsistency is detected by counting each tab as one space.

In *Python 2.X*, combinations of tabs and spaces are allowed, if they satisfy just rule 1; however, mixing tabs and spaces is discouraged, as it is error prone and degrades clarity, and -t or -tt options can be used to flag combinations considered inconsistent per rule 2 (see "Python Command-Line Usage"). In *Python 3.X*, combinations of tabs and spaces are still allowed if they are valid and consistent per *both* rules 1 and 2, but are otherwise always errors (the same as 2.X's -tt option).

For example, in both 3.X and 2.X, an outer block indented with 2 spaces, 1 tab, and 2 spaces (rule 1: 10, rule 2: 5) allows an inner block indented with 1 tab and 5 spaces (rule 1: 13, rule 2: 6). An inner block with 2 tabs and 1 space (rule 1: 17, rule 2: 3) works in 2.X by default (rule 1) but fails in 3.X (rule 2). Maintainable code should not generally rely on these subtle rules: use tabs XOR spaces.

Statements
A statement ends at the end of a line, but can continue over multiple lines if a physical line ends with a \; an unclosed (), [], or {} pair; or an unclosed, triple-quoted string. Multiple simple statements can appear on a single line if they are separated with a semicolon (;).

Comments
Comments start with a # in any column (and not in a string constant) and span to the end of the line; they are ignored by the Python interpreter.

Documentation strings
If a function, module file, or class begins with a string literal (possibly after # comments), it is stored in the object's

__doc__ attribute. See help() in "Built-in Functions", and the pydoc module and script in the Python Library Reference, for automated extraction and display tools. Hint: as of Python 3.2, python -m pydoc -b launches *PyDoc*'s browser-based interface (use -g instead of -b in earlier releases for GUI mode).

Whitespace

Generally significant only to the left of code, where indentation is used to group blocks. Blank lines and spaces are otherwise ignored and optional except as token separators and within string constants.

Name Rules

This section contains the rules for user-defined names (i.e., *variables*) in programs.

Name format

Structure

User-defined names start with a letter or underscore (_), followed by any number of letters, digits, or underscores.

Reserved words

User-defined names cannot be the same as any Python reserved word listed in Table 12.[3]

Case sensitivity

User-defined names and reserved words are always case-sensitive: *SPAM*, *spam*, and *Spam* are different names.

Unused tokens

Python does not use the characters $ and ? in its syntax, although they can appear in string constants and comments. Within strings, $ is special in template substitution (see

---

3. But this rule may be neither absolute nor strict outside the CPython implementation. The Jython Java-based system, for example, may allow reserved words to be used as variables in some contexts.

"Template string substitution"), and $ and ? are special in pattern matching (see "The re Pattern-Matching Module").

Creation

User-defined names are created by assignment but must exist when referenced (e.g., counters must be explicitly initialized to zero). See the sections "Atomic terms and dynamic typing" and "Namespace and Scope Rules".

Table 12. Python 3.X reserved words

False	class	finally	is	return
None	continue	for	lambda	try
True	def	from	nonlocal	while
and	del	global	not	with
as	elif	if	or	yield
assert	else	import	pass	
break	except	in	raise	

NOTE

In Python 2.X, print *and* exec *are both reserved words, as they take the form of statements, not built-in functions. Also in Python 2.X,* nonlocal, True, *and* False *are not reserved words; the first of these is unavailable, and the latter two are simply built-in names.* with *and* as *are reserved as of both 2.6 and 3.0, but not in earlier 2.X releases unless context managers are explicitly enabled.* yield *is reserved as of 2.3; it morphed from statement to expression later but is still a reserved word.*

Name conventions

- Names that begin and end with two underscores (for example, __init__) have a special meaning to the interpreter but are not reserved words.

- Names beginning with one underscore (e.g., _X) and assigned at the top level of a module are not copied out by from...* imports (see also the __all__ module export names list in the sections "The from Statement" and "Pseudoprivate Attributes"). In other contexts, this is an informal convention for internal names.

- Names beginning but not ending with two underscores (e.g., __X) within a class statement are prefixed with the enclosing class's name (see "Pseudoprivate Attributes").

- The name that is just a single underscore (_) is used in the interactive interpreter (only) to store the result of the last evaluation.

- Built-in function and exception names (e.g., open, SyntaxError) are not reserved words. They live in the last-searched scope and can be reassigned to hide (a.k.a. *shadow*) the built-in meaning in the current scope (e.g., open = myfunction).

- Class names commonly begin with an uppercase letter (e.g., MyClass), and modules with a lowercase letter (e.g., mymodule).

- The first (leftmost) argument in a class method function is usually named self, by very strong convention.

- Module names are resolved according to a directory search path scan; names located earlier on the path can hide others of the same name, whether intended or not (see "The import Statement").

Specific Statements

The following sections describe all Python statements. Each section lists the statement's syntax formats, followed by usage details. For compound statements, each appearance of a *suite* in a statement format stands for one or more other statements, possibly indented as a block under a header line. A suite must be indented under a header if it contains another compound statement (`if`, `while`, etc.); otherwise, it can appear on the same line as the statement header. The following are both valid constructs:

```
if x < 42:
    print(x)
    while x: x = x - 1

if x < 42: print(x)
```

The following subsections give details common to both Python 3.X and 2.X; see also "Python 2.X Statements" at the end of this section for details unique to 2.X.

The Assignment Statement

```
target = expression
target1 = target2 = expression
target1, target2 = expression1, expression2
target1 += expression

target1, target2, ...  = same-length-iterable
(target1, target2, ...) = same-length-iterable
[target1, target2, ...] = same-length-iterable
target1, *target2, ...  = matching-length-iterable
```

All assignments store *references* to objects in targets. Assignment statements request assignment with the preceding explicit syntax formats, in which:

- *Expressions* produce objects.

- *Targets* can be simple names (*X*), qualified attributes (*X.attr*), or indexes and slices (*X*[*i*], *X*[*i*:*j*:*k*]).

- *Variables* in targets are not declared ahead of time, but must have been assigned before being used in an expression (see "Atomic terms and dynamic typing").

The first format listed above is *basic* assignment. The second format, *multiple-target* assignment, assigns the same expression result object to each target. The third format, *tuple* assignment, pairs targets with expressions, left to right. The fourth format, *augmented* assignment, is shorthand for an operation plus an assignment (see the next section).

The last four formats are *sequence* assignment, and assign components of any sequence or other iterable to corresponding targets, from left to right. The iterable on the right can be any type, but must be the same length unless a single starred-name (*x*) appears in the targets on the left, as in the last format. This last format, known as *extended sequence* assignment and available in Python 3.X only, allows the starred name to collect arbitrarily many items (see "Extended sequence assignment (3.X)").[4]

Assignment also occurs *implicitly* in other contexts in Python (e.g., for loop variables and function argument passing), and some assignment statement formats apply elsewhere (e.g., sequences in for).

Augmented assignment

A set of additional assignment statement formats, listed in Table 13, are available. Known as *augmented assignments*, these formats imply a binary expression plus an assignment. For instance, the following two formats are roughly equivalent:

```
X = X + Y
X += Y
```

However, the reference to target *X* in the second format needs to be evaluated only *once*, and *in-place* operations may be applied for mutables as an optimization (e.g., *list1 += list2* automatically calls *list1*.extend(*list2*), instead of the slower concatenation operation implied by +). Classes can overload in-place assignments with method names that begin with an i (e.g., __iadd__() for +=, __add__() for +). The format *X //= Y* (floor division) was added as of version 2.2.

---

4. Sequence assignment also allows a nested collection of values to be assigned to a nested sequence of targets: ((a,b),c)=([1,2],3). In Python 2.X only, this pattern may also be used for function header arguments.

Table 13. Augmented assignment statements

$X+=Y$	$X\&=Y$	$X-=Y$	$X|=Y$
$X*=Y$	$X^=Y$	$X/=Y$	$X>>=Y$
$X\%=Y$	$X<<=Y$	$X**=Y$	$X//=Y$

Normal sequence assignment

In Python 2.X and 3.X, any sequence or other iterable of values may be assigned to any sequence of names, as long as the lengths are the same. This basic sequence assignment form works in most assignment contexts:

```
>>> a, b, c, d = [1, 2, 3, 4]
>>> a, d
(1, 4)

>>> for (a, b, c) in [[1, 2, 3], [4, 5, 6]]:
...     print(a, b, c)
...
1 2 3
4 5 6
```

Extended sequence assignment (3.X)

In Python 3.X (only), sequence assignment is extended to allow collection of arbitrarily many items, by prefixing one variable in the assignment target with a star; when used, sequence lengths need not match, and the starred name collects all otherwise unmatched items in a new list:

```
>>> a, *b = [1, 2, 3, 4]
>>> a, b
(1, [2, 3, 4])

>>> a, *b, c = (1, 2, 3, 4)
>>> a, b, c
(1, [2, 3], 4)

>>> *a, b = 'spam'
>>> a, b
```

```
(['s', 'p', 'a'], 'm')

>>> for (a, *b) in [[1, 2, 3], [4, 5, 6]]:
...     print(a, b)
...
1 [2, 3]
4 [5, 6]
```

NOTE

Python 3.5 or later star generalization? In Python 3.3 and
earlier, the special *X and **X syntax forms can appear in
three places: in *assignment statements*, where a *X collects
unmatched items in sequence assignments; in *function
headers*, where the two forms collect unmatched positional
and keyword arguments; and in *function calls*, where the
two forms unpack iterables and dictionaries into individual
items (arguments).

In Python 3.4, developers considered generalizing this star
syntax to also be usable within *data structure literals*—
where it would unpack collections into individual items,
much like its original use in function calls. Specifically, the
unpacking star syntax may be allowed to appear in *tuples*,
lists, *sets*, *dictionaries*, and *comprehensions*. For example:

```
[x, *iter]              # unpack iter items: list
(x, *iter), {x, *iter}  # same for tuple, set
{'x': 1, **dict}        # unpack dict items: dicts
[*iter for iter in x]   # unpack iter items: comps
```

This is in addition to its original three roles in assignment
statements, and function headers and calls. Some current
restrictions regarding use of the star syntax may also be lif-
ted in the process. This proposed change was postponed
until after 3.4 just before this edition was published and
remains uncertain—indeed, it has been debated since 2008,
won't be reconsidered until Python 3.5 or later, and may
never appear at all—so check Python "What's New" documents for more details.

```
```

The Expression Statement

```
expression
function([value, name=value, *name, **name...])
object.method([value, name=value, *name, **name...])
```

Any expression can appear as a statement (e.g., on a line by itself). Conversely, statements cannot appear in any other expression context (e.g., assignment statements have no result, and cannot be nested).

Expression statements are commonly used for calling functions and methods having no useful return value, and for interactive-mode printing. Expression statements are also the most common coding for yield expressions and Python 3.X print() built-in function calls, although both are documented as specific statements in this book.

Call syntax

In function and method calls, actual arguments are separated by commas and are normally matched to arguments in function def headers by position. Calls can optionally list specific argument names in functions to receive passed values by using the *name=value* keyword argument syntax. Keyword arguments match by name instead of position.

Arbitrary arguments call syntax

Special star syntax can also be used in function and method call argument lists to *unpack* collections into arbitrarily many individual arguments. If *pargs* and *kargs* are an iterable and a dictionary, respectively:

```
f(*pargs, **kargs)
```

Then this format calls function f with *positional* arguments from iterable *pargs*, and *keyword* arguments from dictionary *kargs*. For instance:

```
>>> def f(a, b, c, d): print(a, b, c, d)
...
```

```
>>> f(*[1, 2], **dict(c=3, d=4))
1 2 3 4
```

This syntax is intended to be symmetric with function header arbitrary-argument syntax such as def f(*pargs, **kargs), which *collects* unmatched arguments. In calls, starred items are unpacked into individual arguments, and may be combined with other positional and keyword arguments in accordance with ordering rules (e.g., g(1, 2, foo=3, bar=4, *pargs, **kargs)).

In Python 2.X, the apply() built-in function achieves a similar effect, but is removed in Python 3.X:

```
apply(f, pargs, kargs)
```

See also "The def Statement", including Table 15, for more call syntax details.

The print Statement

In Python 3.X, printing text to the standard output stream takes the form of a built-in function call, which is commonly coded as an expression statement (e.g., on a line by itself). Its call signature is as follows:

```
print([value [, value]*]
      [, sep=str] [, end=str]
      [, file=object] [, flush=bool])
```

Each *value* is an expression that produces an object, whose str() string is to be printed. This call is configured by its four optional keyword-only arguments (defaults apply if omitted or passed None):

sep

A string to place between values (default is space: ' ').

end

A string to place at the end of the text printed (default is newline: '\n').

file

> The file-like object to which text is written (default is standard output: sys.stdout).

flush

> Passed true/false, to enable/disable forced output stream flush (as of Python 3.3; default is False).

Pass empty or custom strings to sep and end to suppress or override space separators and line feeds. Pass a file or file-like object to file to redirect output in your script (see also "Files"):

```
>>> print(2 ** 32, 'spam')
4294967296 spam

>>> print(2 ** 32, 'spam', sep='')
4294967296spam

>>> print(2 ** 32, 'spam', end=' '); print(1, 2, 3)
4294967296 spam 1 2 3

>>> print(2 ** 32, 'spam', sep='',
...                    file=open('out', 'w'))
>>> open('out').read()
'4294967296spam\n'
```

Because by default print operations simply call the write() method of the object currently referenced by sys.stdout, the following is equivalent to print(X):

```
import sys
sys.stdout.write(str(X) + '\n')
```

To redirect print text to files or class objects, either pass any object with a write() method to the file keyword argument as shown earlier, or reassign sys.stdout to any such object (see also "Files"):

```
sys.stdout = open('log', 'a')   # Object with write()
print('Warning-bad spam!')      # To object's write()
```

Because sys.stdout can be reassigned, the file keyword argument is not strictly needed; however, it can often avoid both explicit write() method calls, and saving and restoring the original sys.stdout value around a redirected print operation when the original stream is still required. For more on the 3.X print(), see also "Built-in Functions".

Python 2.X print statements

In Python 2.X, printing is a specific statement instead of a built-in function, of the following form:

```
print [value [, value]* [,]]
print >> file [, value [, value]* [,]]
```

The Python 2.X print statement displays the printable representation of each *value* on the standard output stream—the current setting of sys.stdout—and adds spaces between values. A trailing comma suppresses the line feed that is normally added at the end of a list, and is equivalent to using end=' ' in Python 3.X's printing function:

```
>>> print 2 ** 32, 'spam'
4294967296 spam

>>> print 2 ** 32, 'spam',; print 1, 2, 3
4294967296 spam 1 2 3
```

The Python 2.X print statement can also name an open output file-like object to be the target of the printed text, instead of sys.stdout:

```
fileobj = open('log', 'a')
print >> fileobj, "Warning-bad spam!"
```

If the file object is None, sys.stdout is used. This Python 2.X >> syntax is equivalent to the file=F keyword argument in Python 3.X. There is no equivalent to sep=S in Python 2.X's statement, although lines can be preformatted and printed as a single item.

Parentheses work in 2.X's print, but create tuples for multiple items. To use the Python 3.X printing function in Python 2.X, run the following in an interactive session or at the top of a script —this can be used both in 2.X (for 3.X forward compatibility), and in 3.X (for 2.X backward compatibility):

```
from __future__ import print_function
```

The if Statement

```
if test:
    suite
[elif test:
    suite]*
[else:
    suite]
```

The if statement selects from among one or more actions (statement blocks). It runs the suite associated with the first if or elif test that is true, or the else suite if all tests are false. The elif and else parts are optional.

The while Statement

```
while test:
    suite
[else:
    suite]
```

The while loop is a general loop that keeps running the first suite while the test at the top is true. It runs the optional else suite once on exit if the loop ends without running into a break statement in the first suite.

The for Statement

```
for target in iterable:
    suite
[else:
    suite]
```

The for loop is a sequence (or other iterable) iteration that assigns items in iterable to target and runs the first suite for each. The for statement runs the optional else suite once on exit if the loop ends without running into a break statement in the first suite. target can be anything that can appear on the left side of an = assignment statement (e.g., for (x, y) in tuplelist).

Since Python 2.2, this works by first trying to obtain an *iterator* object I with iter(*iterable*) and then calling that object's I.__next__() method repeatedly until StopIteration is raised (I.__next__() is named I.next() in Python 2.X). If no iterator object can be obtained (e.g., no __iter__ method is defined), this works instead by repeatedly indexing *iterable* at successively higher offsets until an IndexError is raised.

Iteration occurs in multiple contexts in Python, including for loop statements, comprehensions, and map(). See "The iteration protocol" in the coverage of lists for more on the mechanism used by the for loop and all other iteration contexts.

The pass Statement

```
pass
```

This is a do-nothing placeholder statement, and is used when syntactically necessary (e.g., for stubbed-out function bodies). In Python 3.X only, ellipses (literally, ...) can achieve similar effects.

The break Statement

```
break
```

This immediately exits the closest (innermost) enclosing while or for loop statement, skipping its associated else (if any). Hint: raise and try statements can be used to exit multiple loop levels.

The continue Statement

```
continue
```

This immediately goes to the top of the closest enclosing while or for loop statement; it resumes in the loop's header line.

The del Statement

```
del name
del name[i]
del name[i:j:k]
del name.attribute
```

The del statement deletes variables, items, keys, slices, and attributes. In the first form, *name* is a variable name taken literally. In the last three forms, *name* can be any expression that evaluates to the subject object (with parentheses if required for priority). For instance: del a.b()[1].c.d.

This statement is primarily for data structures, not memory management. It also removes a reference to formerly referenced objects, which may cause them to be *garbage collected* (reclaimed) if not referenced elsewhere. However, garbage collection is automatic, and need not normally be forced with del.

The def Statement

```
[decoration]
def name([arg,... arg=value,... *arg, **arg]):
    suite
```

The def statement makes new functions, which may also serve as methods in classes. It creates a function object and assigns it to variable *name*. Each call to a function object generates a new, local scope, where assigned names are local to the function call by default (unless declared global, or nonlocal in 3.X). For more on scopes, see "Namespace and Scope Rules".

Arguments are passed by assignment; in a def header, they can be defined by any of the four formats in Table 14. The argument forms in Table 14 can also be used in a function call, where they are interpreted as shown in Table 15 (see "The Expression Statement" for more on function call syntax).

Table 14. Argument formats in definitions

Argument format	Interpretation
name	Matched by name or position
name=value	Default value if *name* is not passed
*name	Collects extra positional arguments as new tuple *name*
**name	Collects extra keyword arguments as a new dictionary *name*

Argument format	Interpretation
`*other, name[=value]`	Python 3.X keyword-only arguments after *
`*, name[=value]`	Same as prior line (when no * otherwise)

Table 15. Argument formats in calls

Argument format	Interpretation
`value`	Positional argument
`name=value`	Keyword (match by name) argument
`*iterable`	Unpacks sequence or other iterable of positional arguments
`**dictionary`	Unpacks dictionary of keyword arguments

Python 3.X keyword-only arguments

Python 3.X (only) generalizes function definition to allow keyword-only arguments, which must be passed by keyword, and are required if not coded with defaults. Keyword-only arguments are coded after the *, which may appear without a name if there are keyword-only arguments but not arbitrary positionals:

```
>>> def f(a, *b, c): print(a, b, c)  # Required kw c
...
>>> f(1, 2, c=3)
1 (2,) 3

>>> def f(a, *, c=None): print(a, c) # Optional kw c
...
>>> f(1)
1 None
>>> f(1, c='spam')
1 spam
```

Python 3.X function annotations

Python 3.X (only) also generalizes function definition to allow arguments and return values to be annotated with object values for use in extensions. Annotations are coded as `:value` after the argument name and before a default, and as `->value` after the argument list. They are collected into an __annotations__ attribute of the function, but are not otherwise treated as special by Python itself:

```
>>> def f(a:99, b:'spam'=None) -> float:
...     print(a, b)
...
>>> f(88)
88 None
>>> f.__annotations__
{'a': 99, 'b': 'spam', 'return': <class 'float'>}
```

lambda expressions

Functions can also be created with the lambda expression form, which creates a new function object and returns it to be called later, instead of assigning it to a name:

```
lambda arg, arg,...: expression
```

In lambda, each *arg* is as in def (Table 14), and *expression* is the implied return value of later calls; code in *expression* is effectively deferred until calls:

```
>>> L = lambda a, b=2, *c, **d: [a, b, c, d]
>>> L(1, 2, 3, 4, x=1, y=2)
[1, 2, (3, 4), {'y': 2, 'x': 1}]
```

Because lambda is an expression, not a statement, it can be used in places that a def cannot (e.g., within a dictionary literal expression or an argument list of a function call). Because lambda computes a single expression instead of running statements, it is not intended for complex functions (use def).

Function defaults and attributes

Mutable default argument values are evaluated once at def statement time, not on each call, and so can retain state between calls. However, some consider this behavior to be a caveat, and classes and enclosing scope references are often better state-retention tools; use None defaults for mutable and explicit tests to avoid unwanted changes, as shown in the following's comments:

```
>>> def grow(a, b=[]):        # def grow(a, b=None):
...        b.append(a)        #     if b == None: b = []
...        print(b)           #     ...
...
>>> grow(1); grow(2)
[1]
[1, 2]
```

Both Python 2.X and 3.X also support attachment of arbitrary *attributes* to functions, as another form of state retention (although attributes support only per-function-object state, which is per-call only if each call generates a new function object):

```
>>> grow.food = 'spam'
>>> grow.food
'spam'
```

Function and method decorators

As of Python 2.4, function definitions can be preceded by a declaration syntax that describes the function that follows. Known as *decorators* and coded with an @ character, these declarations provide explicit syntax for functional techniques. The function decorator syntax:

```
@decorator
def F():
    ...
```

is equivalent to this manual name rebinding:

```
def F():
    ...
F = decorator(F)
```

The effect is to rebind the function name to the result of passing the function through the *decorator* callable. Function decorators may be used to manage functions, or later calls made to them (by using proxy objects). Decorators may be applied to any function definition, including methods inside a class:

```
class C:
    @decorator
    def M():              # Same as M = decorator(M)
        ...
```

More generally, the following nested decoration:

```
@A
@B
@C
def f(): ...
```

is equivalent to the following nondecorator code:

```
def f(): ...
f = A(B(C(f)))
```

Decorators may also take argument lists:

```
@spam(1, 2, 3)
def f(): ...
```

In this case, spam must be a function returning a function, and is known as a *factory function*; its result is used as the actual decorator, and may retain argument state as needed. Decorators must appear on the line preceding a function definition, not the same line (e.g., @A def f(): ... on a single line is illegal).

Because they accept and return callables, some built-in functions, including property(), staticmethod(), and classmethod(), may be used as function decorators (see "Built-in Functions"). Decorator syntax is also supported for *classes* in Python 2.6 and 3.0, and later in both lines; see "The class Statement".

The return Statement

```
return [expression]
```

The return statement exits the enclosing function and returns an *expression* value as the result of the call to the function. If *expression* is omitted, it defaults to None, which is also the default return value for functions that exit without a return. Hint: return a tuple for multiple-value function results. See also "The yield

---

Statement" for special semantics of return when used in a generator function.

The yield Statement

```
yield expression        # All Pythons
yield from iterable     # 3.3 and later
```

The yield expression in 2.X and 3.X defines a *generator function*, which produces results on demand. Functions containing a yield are compiled specially; when called, they create and return a *generator object*—an iterable that automatically supports the *iteration protocol* to provide results in iteration contexts.

Commonly coded as an expression statement (e.g., on a line by itself), yield suspends function state and returns an *expression* value. On the next iteration, the function's prior location and variable state are restored, and control resumes immediately after the yield statement.

Use a return statement to end the iteration or simply fall off the end of the function. A generator function return must give no return value prior to 3.3, but may provide one in 3.3 and later that is retained as an exception object attribute (see "Generator function changes in Python 3.3"):

```
def generateSquares(N):
    for i in range(N):
        yield i ** 2

>>> G = generateSquares(5)  # Has __init__, __next__
>>> list(G)                 # Generate results now
[0, 1, 4, 9, 16]
```

When used as an expression (e.g., A = yield X), yield returns the object passed to the generator's send() method at the caller, and must be enclosed in parenthesis unless it is the only item on the right of = (e.g., A = (yield X) + 42). In this mode, values are sent to a generator by calling send(*value*); the generator is resumed, and the yield expression returns *value*. If the regular __next__() method or next() built-in function is called to advance, yield returns None.

Generator functions also have a `throw(type)` method to raise an exception inside the generator at the latest `yield`, and a `close()` method that raises a new `GeneratorExit` exception inside the generator to terminate the iteration. `yield` is standard as of version 2.3 and later; generator `send()`, `throw()`, and `close()` methods are available as of Python 2.5.

A class `__iter__()` method containing a `yield` returns a generator with an automatically created `__next__()`. See "The iteration protocol" in the coverage of lists for the mechanism used by generator functions, and "Generator expressions" for a related tool which also creates a generator object.

Generator function changes in Python 3.3

As of 3.3, Python 3.X (only) supports a `from` clause in this statement, which in basic usage is similar to a yielding `for` loop that steps through items in an *iterable*; in more advanced roles, this extension allows subgenerators to receive sent and thrown values directly from the higher calling scope:

```
for i in range(N): yield i    # All Pythons
yield from range(N)           # 3.3 and later option
```

Also as of 3.3, if a generator function stops iteration and exits with an explicit `return` statement, any value given in the `return` is made available as the `value` attribute of the implicitly created and raised `StopIteration` instance object. This value is ignored by automatic iterations, but may be queried by manual iterations or other code that accesses the exception (see "Built-in Exceptions"). In Python 2.X, and in 3.X prior to 3.3, a `return` with a value in a generator function is treated as a syntax error.

The global Statement

```
global name [, name]*
```

The `global` statement is a namespace declaration: when used inside a class or function definition statement, it causes all appearances of *name* in that context to be treated as references to a global

(module-level) variable of that name—whether name is assigned
or not, and whether name already exists or not.

This statement allows globals to be created or changed within a
function or class. Because of Python's scope rules, you need to
declare only global names that are *assigned*; undeclared names
are made local if assigned, but global references are automatically
located in the enclosing module. See also "Namespace and Scope
Rules".

The nonlocal Statement

```
nonlocal name [, name]*
```

Available in Python 3.X only.

The nonlocal statement is a namespace declaration: when used
inside a nested function, it causes all appearances of *name* in that
context to be treated as references to a local variable of that name
in an enclosing function's scope—whether name is assigned or not.

name must exist in an enclosing function; this statement allows it
to be changed by a nested function. Because of Python's scope
rules, you need to declare only nonlocal names that are *assigned*; undeclared names are made local if assigned, but nonlocal
references are automatically located in enclosing functions. See
also "Namespace and Scope Rules".

The import Statement

```
import [package.]* module [as name]
        [, [package.]* module [as name]]*
```

The import statement provides module access: it imports a module as a whole. Modules in turn contain names fetched by qualification: *module.attribute*. Assignments at the top level of a
Python file create module object attributes. The optional as
clause assigns a variable *name* to the imported module object and
removes the original *module* name (useful to provide shorter syn-
onyms for long module names or package paths), and optional

package prefixes denote package directory paths (described in the next section).

module names the target *module*, which is usually a Python source-code or compiled byte-code file. The *module* is given without its filename extension (e.g., *.py*), and must generally be located in a directory on the module search path unless nested in a *package* path.

For the leftmost *module* or *package* components in absolute import paths, the *module search path* is sys.path—a directory name list initialized from the program's top-level directory, PYTHONPATH settings, .pth path file contents, and Python defaults. Modules may instead be located in a single package directory for nested package components (see "Package imports") and relative imports in from statements (see "Package relative import syntax"), and search paths may span directories arbitrarily for namespace packages as of Python 3.3 (see "Python 3.3 namespace packages").

The first time a module is imported by a program, its source-code file is compiled to *byte code* if needed (and saved in a *.pyc* file if possible), and then executed from top to bottom to generate module object attributes by assignment. In Python 2.X and 3.1 and earlier, byte-code files are saved in the source-code file's directory with the same base name (e.g., *module.pyc*). In Python 3.2 and later, byte code is saved in a *__pycache__* subdirectory of the source-code file's directory, with a version-identifying base name (e.g., *module.cpython-33.pyc*).

Later imports use the already-imported module, but imp.reload() (reload() in 2.X) forces reimports of already-loaded modules. To import by string name, see __import__() used by import in "Built-in Functions" and the standard library's importlib.import_module(*modname*).

In standard CPython, imports may also load compiled C and C++ extensions, with attributes corresponding to external language names. In other implementations, imports may also name other language's class libraries (e.g., Jython may generate a Python module wrapper that interfaces with a Java library).

Package imports

If used, the *package* prefix names give enclosing directory names, and module dotted paths reflect directory hierarchies. An import of the form `import dir1.dir2.mod` generally loads the module file at directory path *dir1/dir2/mod.py*, where *dir1* must be contained by a directory listed on the module search path (`sys.path` for absolute imports) and *dir2* is located in *dir1* (not on `sys.path`).

In regular packages, each directory listed in an import statement must have a (possibly empty) *__init__.py* file that serves as the directory level's module namespace. This file is run on the first import through the directory, and all names assigned in *__init__.py* files become attributes of the directory's module object. Directory packages can resolve same-name conflicts caused by the linear nature of `PYTHONPATH`.

See also "Package relative import syntax" for more on intra-package references in `from` statements, and "Python 3.3 namespace packages" for an alternative package type which requires no *__init__.py* file.

Python 3.3 namespace packages

As of Python 3.3, the import operation is extended to recognize *namespace packages*—module packages that are the virtual concatenation of one or more directories nested in module search path entries.

Namespace packages do not (and cannot) contain an *__init__.py* file. They serve as a fallback option and extension to regular modules and packages, recognized only if a name is not located otherwise but matches one or more directories found during the search path scan. This feature is activated by both the `import` and `from` statements.

Import algorithm

With the addition of namespaces packages, imports follow their usual initial steps as before (e.g., checking for already-imported modules and byte-code files), but the search for a module is extended as follows.

During imports, Python iterates over each directory in the *module search path*—defined by `sys.path` for the leftmost components of absolute imports, and by a package's location for relative imports and components nested in package paths. As of 3.3, while looking for an imported module or package named *spam*, for each *directory* in the module search path, Python tests for matching criteria in this order (where step 2 involves details omitted here, including the 3.2 *__pycache__* subdirectory described earlier):

1. If *directory\spam__init__.py* is found, a *regular package* is imported and returned.

2. If *directory\spam.{py, pyc, or other module extension}* is found, a simple *module* is imported and returned.

3. If *directory\spam* is found and is a directory, it is recorded and the scan continues with the next directory in the search path.

4. If none of the above was found, the scan continues with the next directory in the search path.

If the search path scan completes without returning a module or package by steps *1* or *2*, and at least one *directory* was recorded by step *3*, then a *namespace package* is immediately created. The new namespace package has a `__path__` attribute set to an iterable of the directory path strings that were found and recorded during the scan by step 3, but does not have a `__file__`.

The `__path__` attribute is used in later accesses to search all package components whenever further nested items are requested, much like the sole directory of a regular package. It serves the same role for lower-level components that `sys.path` does at the top for the leftmost components of absolute import paths, becoming the parent path for accessing lower items using the same four-step algorithm.

The from Statement

```
from [package.]* module import
            [() name [as othername]
            [, name [as othername]]* [)]

from [package.]* module import *
```

The from statement imports a module just as in the import statement (see the preceding section), but also copies variable names from the module to be used without qualification: *attribute.* The second format (from ... import *) copies *all* names assigned at the top level of the module, except those with a single leading underscore or not listed in the module's __all__ list-of-strings attribute (if defined).

If used, the as clause creates a name synonym as in the import statement, and works for any *name* component. If used, *package* import paths also work as in import (e.g., from *dir1.dir2.mod* import *X*) for both regular and 3.3 namespace packages, although the package path needs to be listed only once in the from itself (not at each attribute reference). As of Python 2.4, the names being imported from a module can be enclosed in parentheses to span multiple lines without backslashes (this is special-case syntax for from only).

In Python 3.X, the from ... import * form is invalid within a function or class, because it makes it impossible to classify name scopes at definition time. Due to scoping rules, the * format also generates warnings in 2.X as of version 2.2 if it appears nested in a function or class.

The from statement is also used to enable future (but still pending) language additions, with from __future__ import *featurename.* This format must appear only at the top of a module file (preceded only by a docstring or comments), or anytime during an interactive session.

Package relative import syntax

In Python 3.X and 2.X, the `from` statement (but *not* `import`) may use leading dots in module names to specify intra-package module references—imports which are *relative* to the package directory in which the importing module resides only. Relative imports restrict the initial module search path to the package directory. Other imports are *absolute*, locating modules on `sys.path`. General syntax patterns:

```
from source import name [, name]*    # Abs: sys.path

from . import module [, module]*     # Rel: pkg only
from .source import name [, name]*   # Rel: pkg only

from .. import module [, module]*    # Parent in pkg
from ..source import name [, name]*  # Parent in pkg
```

In this `from` form, *source* may be a simple identifier or dot-separated package path, *name* and *module* are simple identifiers, and leading dots identify the import as package relative. The `as` renaming extension (not shown here) also works in this form as in normal `from` for both *name* and *module*.

Leading-dots syntax works in both Python 3.X and 2.X to make imports explicitly package relative. However, for imports *without* leading dots, the package's own directory is searched first in Python 2.X, but not in Python 3.X. To enable full Python 3.X package import semantics in Python 2.6 and later, use:

```
from __future__ import absolute_import
```

Because they may support a broader range of use cases, absolute package import paths, relative to a directory on `sys.path`, are often preferred over both implicit package-relative imports in Python 2.X, and explicit package-relative import syntax in both Python 2.X and 3.X.

The class Statement

```
[decoration]
class name [ ( super [, super]* [, metaclass=M] ) ]:
    suite
```

The class statement makes new class objects, which are factories for making instance objects. The new class object inherits from each listed *super* class in the order given, and is assigned to variable *name*. The class statement introduces a new local name scope, and all names assigned in the class statement generate class object attributes shared by all instances of the class.

Important class features include the following; for further class and OOP details, see also the sections "Object-Oriented Programming" and "Operator Overloading Methods":

- *Superclasses* (also known as base classes) from which a new class inherits attributes are listed in parentheses in the header (e.g., class Sub(Super1, Super2)).

- Assignments in the statement's suite generate *class attributes* inherited by instances: nested def statements make *methods*, while assignment statements make simple class members.

- Calling the class generates *instance objects*. Each instance object may have its own attributes, and inherits the attributes of the class and all of its superclasses.

- *Method functions* receive a special first argument, called self by very strong convention, which is the instance object that is the implied subject of the method call, and gives access to instance state information attributes.

- The staticmethod() and classmethod() built-ins support additional kinds of methods, and Python 3.X methods may be treated as simple functions when called through a class.

- Specially named _*X*_ *operator overloading* methods intercept built-in operations.

- Where warranted, classes provide state retention and program structure, and support *code reuse* through customization in new classes.

Class decorators in Python 3.X, 2.6, and 2.7

In Python 2.6, 3.0, and later in both lines, decorator syntax can be applied to class statements, in addition to function definitions. The class decorator syntax:

```
@decorator
class C:
    def meth():
        ...
```

is equivalent to this manual name rebinding:

```
class C:
    def meth():
        ...
C = decorator(C)
```

The effect is to rebind the class name to the result of passing the class through the *decorator* callable. Like function decorators, class decorators may be nested and support decorator arguments. Class decorators may be used to manage classes, or later instance-creation calls made to them (by using proxy objects).

Metaclasses

Metaclasses are classes that generally subclass from the type class, in order to customize creation of class objects themselves. For example:

```
class Meta(type):
    def __new__(meta, cname, supers, cdict):
        # This and __init__ run by type.__call__
        c = type.__new__(meta, cname, supers, cdict)
        return c
```

In Python 3.X, classes define their metaclasses using keyword arguments in class headers:

```
class C(metaclass=Meta): ...
```

In Python 2.X, use class attributes instead:

```
class C(object):
    __metaclass__ = Meta
    ...
```

Metaclass code is run at the conclusion of a class statement (much like class decorators). See also type() in "Built-in Functions" for the mapping from class statements to metaclass methods.

The try Statement

```
try:
    suite
except [type [as value]]:      # Or [, value] in 2.X
    suite
[except [type [as value]]:
    suite]*
[else:
    suite]
[finally:
    suite]

try:
    suite
finally:
    suite
```

The try statement catches exceptions. try statements can specify except clauses with suites that serve as handlers for exceptions raised during the try suite; else clauses that run if no exception occurs during the try suite; and finally clauses that run whether an exception happens or not. except clauses catch and recover from exceptions, and finally clauses run termination (block exit) actions.

Exceptions can be raised automatically by Python, or explicitly by code in raise statements (see "The raise Statement"). In except clauses, type is an expression giving the exception class to be caught, and an extra variable name *value* can be used to intercept the instance of the exception class that was raised. Table 16 lists all the clauses that can appear in a `try` statement.

The `try` must have either an `except` or a `finally`, or both. The order of its parts must be: `try`→`except`→`else`→`finally`, where the `else` and `finally` are optional, and there may be zero or more `except` clauses, but there must be at least one `except` if an `else` appears. `finally` interacts correctly with `return`, `break`, and `continue`: if any of these pass control out of the `try` block, the `finally` clause is executed on the way out.

Table 16. try statement clause formats

Clause format	Interpretation
`except:`	Catch all (or all other) exceptions
`except` *type*:	Catch a specific exception only
`except` *type* as *value*:	Catch exception and its instance
`except` (*type1*, *type2*):	Catch any of the exceptions
`except` (*type1*, *type2*) as *value*:	Catch any of the exceptions and its instance
`else:`	Run if no exceptions are raised
`finally:`	Always run this block on the way out

Common variations include the following:

`except` *classname* as *X*:
> Catch a class exception, and assign *X* to the raised instance. *X* gives access to any attached state information attributes, print strings, or callable methods on the instance raised. For older string exceptions, *X* is assigned to the extra data passed along with the string (string exceptions are removed in both Python 3.X and 2.X, as of 3.0 and 2.6).

`except` (*type1*, *type2*, *type3*) as *X*:
> Catch any of the exceptions named in a tuple, and assign *X* to the extra data.

In Python 3.X, the name *X* in the as clause is *localized* to the except block, and removed when it exits; in 2.X, this name is not local to this block. See also the sys.exc_info() call in "The sys Module" for generic access to the exception class and instance (a.k.a., *type* and *value*) after an exception is raised.

Python 2.X try statement forms

In Python 2.X, try statements work as described, but the as clause used in except handlers to access the raised instance is coded with a comma instead—both as and comma work in 2.6 and 2.7 (for 3.X compatibility), but as is not present in earlier 2.X:

```
except classname, X:
```
> Catch a class exception, and assign *X* to the raised instance (use as after 2.5).

```
except (name1, name2, name2), X:
```
> Catch any of the exceptions, and assign *X* to the extra data (use as after 2.5).

The raise Statement

In Python 3.X, the raise statement takes the following forms:

```
raise instance [from (otherexc | None)]
raise class    [from (otherexc | None)]
raise
```

The first form raises a manually created instance of a class (e.g., raise Error(args)). The second form creates and raises a new instance of *class* (equivalent to raise *class*()). The third form reraises the most recent exception. See the next section ("Python 3.X chained exceptions") for the optional from clause.

The raise statement triggers exceptions. It may be used to explicitly raise either built-in exceptions or user-defined exceptions. See also "Built-in Exceptions" for exceptions predefined by Python.

On raise, control jumps to the matching except clause of the most recently entered try statement whose clause matches, or, if none match, to the top level of the process where it ends the program and prints a standard error message. Any `finally` clauses are run along the way. An `except` clause is considered matching if it names the raised instance's class, or one of its superclasses (see "Class exceptions"). The instance object raised is assigned to the `as` variable in the matching `except` clause (if given).

Python 3.X chained exceptions

In Python 3.X (only), the optional `from` clause allows exception chaining: *otherexc* is another exception class or instance, and is attached to the raised exception's `__cause__` attribute. If the raised exception is not caught, Python prints both exceptions as part of the standard error message:

```
try:
    ...
except Exception as E:
    raise TypeError('Bad') from E
```

As of Python 3.3, the `raise from` form can also specify `None`, to cancel any chained exceptions accumulated to the point of the statement's execution:

```
raise TypeError('Bad') from None
```

Class exceptions

As of Python 3.0 and 2.6, all exceptions are identified by classes, which must be derived from the built-in `Exception` class (in 2.X, this derivation is required of new-style classes only). The `Exception` superclass provides defaults for display strings, as well as constructor argument retention in tuple attribute `args`.

Class exceptions support exception *categories*, which can be easily extended. Because `try` statements catch all subclasses when they name a superclass, exception categories can be modified by altering the set of subclasses without breaking existing `try` statements. The raised instance object also provides storage for extra information about the exception:

```
class General(Exception):
    def __init__(self, x):
        self.data = x

class Specific1(General): pass
class Specific2(General): pass

try:
    raise Specific1('spam')
except General as X:
    print(X.data)                # Prints 'spam'
```

Python 2.X raise statement forms

Prior to Python 2.6, Python 2.X allows exceptions to be identified
with both strings and classes. Because of this, its raise statements
may take the following forms, many of which exist for backward
compatibility:

```
raise string             # Match same string object
raise string, data       # Assign data to exc var

raise class, instance    # Match class or any super
raise instance           # = inst.__class__, inst

raise class              # = class()
raise class, arg         # = class(arg), noninst
raise class, (arg [, arg]*) # = class(arg, arg,...)
raise                    # Re-raise current exc
```

String exceptions were deprecated as of (and issue warnings in)
Python 2.5. Python 2.X also allows a third item in raise statements, which must be a traceback object used instead of the current location as the place where the exception occurred.

The assert Statement

```
assert expression [, message]
```

The assert statement performs debugging checks. If *expression*
is false, it raises AssertionError, passing it *message* as its

constructor argument, if provided. The -O command-line flag
removes assertions (their tests are neither included nor run).

The with Statement

```
with expression [as variable]:           # 3.0/2.6, +
    suite

with expression [as variable]
        [, expression [as variable]]*:   # 3.1/2.7, +
    suite
```

The with statement wraps a nested block of code in a context
manager (described ahead), which can run block entry actions,
and ensure that block exit actions are run whether exceptions are
raised or not. with can be an alternative to try/finally for exit
actions, but only for objects having context managers.

expression is assumed to return an object that supports the context management protocol. This object may also return a value
that will be assigned to the name *variable* if the optional as clause
is present. Classes may define custom context managers, and
some built-in types such as files and threads provide context
managers with exit actions that close files, release thread locks,
etc.:

```
with open(r'C:\misc\script', 'w') as myfile:
    ...process myfile, auto-closed on suite exit...
```

See "Files" for more details on file context manager usage, and
Python manuals for other built-in types that support this protocol and statement.

This statement is supported as of Python 2.6 and 3.0, and may be
enabled in 2.5 with the following:

```
from __future__ import with_statement
```

Multiple context managers in Python 3.1 and 2.7

As of Python 3.1 and 2.7, the with statement may also specify multiple (a.k.a. *nested*) context managers. Any number of context manager items may be separated by commas, and multiple items work the same as nested with statements. In general, this code in 3.1, 2.7, and later:

```
with A() as a, B() as b:
    ...statements...
```

is equivalent to the following, which also works in 3.0 and 2.6:

```
with A() as a:
    with B() as b:
        ...statements...
```

For example, in the following code, both files' exit actions are automatically run when the statement block exits, regardless of exception outcomes:

```
with open('data') as fin, open('res', 'w') as fout:
    for line in fin:
        fout.write(transform(line))
```

Context manager protocol

Objects integrate with the with statement according to the following method-call model; see also "Methods for Context Managers":

1. The *expression* is evaluated, resulting in an object known as a context manager that must define method names __enter__ and __exit__.

2. The context manager's __enter__() method is called. The value it returns is assigned to *variable* if present, or simply discarded otherwise.

3. The code in the nested *suite* is executed.

4. If the *suite* raises an exception, the __exit__(*type*, *value*, *traceback*) method is called with the exception details. If this method returns a false value, the exception is reraised; otherwise, the exception is terminated.

5. If the *suite* does not raise an exception, the __exit__ method is still called, but its three arguments are all passed in as None.

Python 2.X Statements

Python 2.X supports the print statement described earlier, does not support nonlocal, and does not support with fully until 2.6. In addition, raise, try, and def have the slightly different syntaxes in Python 2.X as noted earlier, and semantics noted as 3.X-specific in the preceding section do not generally apply to 2.X (e.g., namespace packages).

The following additional statement is available in Python 2.X only:

```
exec codestring [in globaldict [, localdict]]
```

The exec statement runs code dynamically. *codestring* may be any Python statement (or multiple statements separated by newlines) as a string, which is compiled and run in the namespace containing the exec, or the global/local namespace dictionaries if specified (*localdict* defaults to *globaldict*). *codestring* can also be a compiled code object. Also see compile(), eval(), and the Python 2.X execfile() in "Built-in Functions".

In Python 3.X, this statement becomes the exec() function (see "Built-in Functions"). The backward- and forward-compatible syntax exec(a, b, c) is also accepted in Python 2.X. Hint: do not use this to evaluate untrustworthy code strings, as they run as program code.

Namespace and Scope Rules

This section discusses rules for name binding and lookup (see also the sections "Name format", "Name conventions", and "Atomic terms and dynamic typing"). In all cases, names are created when first assigned but must already exist when referenced. Qualified and unqualified names are resolved differently.

Qualified Names: Object Namespaces

Qualified names— *X*, in *object.X*—are known as *attributes* and live in object namespaces. Assignments in some lexical scopes[5] serve to initialize object namespaces (e.g., module and class attributes):

Assignment: object.X = value
> Creates or alters the attribute name *X* in the namespace of the *object*. This is the normal case; see "Formal Inheritance Rules" ahead for full details.

Reference: object.X
> Searches for the attribute name *X* in the *object*, and then all accessible classes above it for instances and classes. This is the definition of *inheritance*; see "Formal Inheritance Rules" for full details.

Unqualified Names: Lexical Scopes

Unqualified names— *X*, at the start of an expression—involve lexical scope rules. Assignments bind such names to the local scope unless they are declared global, or nonlocal in 3.X.

Assignment: X = value
> Makes name *X* local by default: creates or changes name *X* in the current local scope. If *X* is declared global, this creates or changes name *X* in the enclosing module's scope. In

---

5. Lexical scopes refer to physically (syntactically) nested code structures in a program's source code.

Python 3.X only, if *X* is declared nonlocal, this changes name *X* in an enclosing function's scope. Local variables are normally stored in the call stack at runtime for quick access, and directly visible only to code in the same scope.

Reference: X

Looks for name *X* in at most four scope categories, in the following order:

a. The current *local* scope (the innermost enclosing function)

b. The local scopes of all lexically *enclosing functions* (other function layers, from inner to outer)

c. The current *global* scope (the enclosing module)

d. The *built-in* scope (which corresponds to module builtins in Python 3.X, and module __builtin__ in Python 2.X)

Local and global scope contexts are defined in Table 17. global declarations make the search begin in the global scope instead, and nonlocal declarations in 3.X restrict the search to enclosing functions.

Special cases: comprehensions, exceptions

Python 3.X localizes loop variables in all *comprehensions* (Python 2.X does the same for all but list comprehensions). Python 3.X localizes and removes the exception variable in the except clause of try statements (2.X does not localize this name). See also "List comprehension expressions" and "The try Statement".

Table 17. Unqualified name scopes

Code context	Global scope	Local scope
Module	Same as local	The module itself
Function, method	Enclosing module	Function definition/call
Class	Enclosing module	class statement

Code context	Global scope	Local scope
Script, interactive mode	Same as local	module __main__
exec(), eval()	Caller's global (or passed in)	Caller's local (or passed in)

Nested Scopes and Closures

The *enclosing functions* search of the previous section's "Reference" rules (step *b*) is called a *statically nested scope*, and was made standard as of version 2.2. For example, the following function works because the reference to x within f2 has access to the enclosing f1 scope:

```
def f1():
    x = 42
    def f2():
        print(x)      # Retain x in f1's scope
    return f2          # To be called later: f1()()=>42
```

Nested functions that retain enclosing scope references (e.g., f2 in the preceding code) are known as *closures*—a state retention tool that is sometimes an alternative or complement to classes, and made more useful in 3.X with nonlocal (see "The nonlocal Statement"). Scopes nest arbitrarily, but only enclosing functions (not classes) are searched:

```
def f1():
    x = 42
    def f2():
        def f3():
            print(x)   # Finds x in f1's scope
        f3()           # f1() prints 42
    f2()
```

Enclosing scopes and defaults

In Python versions prior to 2.2, the preceding section's functions fail because name x is not local (in the nested function's scope), global (in the module enclosing f1), or built-in. To make such cases work prior to version 2.2 or when required otherwise, *default arguments* retain values from the immediately enclosing scope, because values of defaults are evaluated before entering a def:

```
def f1():
    x = 42
    def f2(x=x):
        print(x)          # f1()() prints 42
    return f2
```

This technique still works in more recent Python versions, and also applies to lambda expressions, which imply a nested scope just like def and are more commonly nested in practice:

```
def func(x):
    action = (lambda n: x ** n)        # Use as of 2.2
    return action                      # func(2)(4)=16

def func(x):
    action = (lambda n, x=x: x ** n) # Defaults alt
    return action                      # func(2)(4)=16
```

Though now largely outdated in most roles, defaults are still sometimes needed to reference *loop variables* when creating functions inside loops; otherwise, such variables reflect only their *final* loop value:

```
for I in range(N):
    actions.append(lambda I=I: F(I))  # Current I
```

Object-Oriented Programming

Classes are Python's main *object-oriented programming* (OOP) tool. They support multiple instances, attribute inheritance, and operator overloading. Python also supports *functional programming* techniques—with tools such as generators, lambdas, comprehensions, maps, closures, decorators, and first-class function objects—which may serve as complement or alternative to OOP in some contexts.

Classes and Instances

Class objects provide default behavior

- The class statement creates a *class* object and assigns it to a name.

- Assignments inside class statements create class *attributes*, which are inherited object state and behavior.

- Class *methods* are nested defs, with special first arguments to receive the implied subject instance.

Instance objects are generated from classes

- Calling a class object like a function makes a new *instance* object.

- Each instance object inherits class attributes and gets its own attribute *namespace*.

- Assignments to attributes of the first argument (e.g., *self.X = V*) in methods create per-instance *attributes*.

Inheritance rules

- Inheritance happens at attribute qualification time: on *object.attribute*, if *object* is a class or instance.

- Classes inherit attributes from all classes listed in their class statement header line (superclasses). Listing more than one means *multiple inheritance*.

- Instances inherit attributes from the class from which they are generated, plus all that class's superclasses.

- Inheritance searches the instance, then its class, then all accessible superclasses, and uses the first version of an attribute name found. Superclasses are normally searched depth-first and then left to right, but new-style classes search across before proceeding up in diamond pattern trees (only).

See "Formal Inheritance Rules" for more details on inheritance.

Pseudoprivate Attributes

By default, all attribute names in modules and classes are visible everywhere. Special conventions allow some limited data hiding but are mostly designed to prevent name collisions (see also "Name conventions").

Module privates

Names in modules with a single underscore (e.g., _X), and those not listed on the module's __all__ list, are not copied over when a client uses from *module* import *. This is not strict privacy, however, as such names can still be accessed with other import statement forms.

Class privates

Names anywhere within class statements with two leading underscores only (e.g., __X) are mangled at compile time to include the enclosing class name as a prefix (e.g., _Class__X). The added class-name prefix localizes such names to the enclosing class and thus makes them distinct in both the *self* instance object and the class hierarchy.

This helps to avoid unintended clashes that may arise for same-named methods, and for attributes in the single instance object at the bottom of the inheritance chain (for a given *attr*, all assignments to *self.attr* anywhere in a framework change the single instance namespace). This is not strict privacy, however, as such attributes can still be accessed via the mangled name.

Privacy-like access control can also be implemented with proxy classes that validate attribute access in __getattr__() and __setattr__() methods (see "Operator Overloading Methods").

New-Style Classes

In Python 3.X, there is a single class model: all classes are considered *new-style* whether they derive from object or not. In Python 2.X, there are two class models: *classic*—the default in all 2.X; and *new-style*—an option in 2.2 and later, coded by deriving from a built-in type or the built-in object class (e.g., class A(object)).

New-style classes (including all classes in Python 3.X) differ from classic classes in the following ways:

- Diamond patterns of multiple inheritances have a slightly different search order—roughly, they are searched across before up, and more breadth-first than depth-first, per the new-style __mro__ (see "Formal Inheritance Rules").

- Classes are now types, and types are now classes. The type(I) built-in returns the class an instance is made from, instead of a generic instance type, and is normally the same as I.__class__. The type class may be subclassed to customize class creation, and all classes inherit from object, which provides a small set of method defaults.

- The __getattr__() and __getattribute__() methods are no longer run for attributes implicitly fetched by built-in operations. They are not called for __X__ operator - overloading method names by built-ins; the search for such names begins at classes, not instances. To intercept and delegate access to such method names, they generally must be redefined in wrapper/proxy classes.

- New-style classes have a set of new class tools, including slots, properties, descriptors, and the __getattribute__() method. Most of these have tool-building purposes. See "Operator Overloading Methods" for __slots__, __getattribute__(), and descriptor __get__(), __set__(), and __delete__() methods; see "Built-in Functions" for property().

Formal Inheritance Rules

Inheritance occurs on attribute name reference—the
`object.name` lookup at the heart of object-oriented code—whenever `object` is derived from a class. It differs in classic and new-
style classes, although typical code often runs the same in both
models.

Classic classes: DFLR

In classic classes (the default in 2.X), for name references, inheritance searches:

1. The *instance*

2. Then its *class*

3. Then all its class's *superclasses*, depth-first and then left to
   right

The first occurrence found along the way is used. This order is
known as *DFLR*.

This reference search may be kicked off from either an instance
or a class; attribute *assignments* normally store in the target object
itself without search; and there are special cases for
`__getattr__()` (run if the lookup failed to find a name) and
`__setattr__()` (run for all attribute assignments).

New-style classes: MRO

Inheritance in new-style classes (the standard in 3.X and an option in 2.X) employ the *MRO*—a linearized path through a class
tree, and a nested component of inheritance, made available in a
class's `__mro__` attribute. The MRO is roughly computed as
follows:

1. List all the classes that an instance inherits from using the
   classic class's DFLR lookup rule, and include a class multiple times if it's visited more than once.

2. Scan the resulting list for duplicate classes, removing all but the last (rightmost) occurrence of duplicates in the list.

The resulting MRO sequence for a given class includes the class, its superclasses, and all higher superclasses up to and including the implicit or explicit object root class at the top of the tree. It's ordered such that each class appears before its parents, and multiple parents retain the order in which they appear in the __bases__ superclass tuple.

Because common parents in *diamonds* appear only at the position of their *last* visitation in the MRO, lower classes are searched first when the MRO list is used later by attribute inheritance (making it more breadth-first than depth-first in diamonds only), and each class is included and thus visited just *once*, no matter how many classes lead to it.

The MRO ordering is used both by inheritance (ahead) and by the super() call—a built-in function that always invokes a *next* class on the MRO (relative to the call point), which might not be a superclass at all, but can be used to dispatch method calls throughout a class tree visiting each class just once.

Example: nondiamonds

```
class D:       attr = 3      #   D:3    E:2
class B(D):    pass          #    |      |
class E:       attr = 2      #    B     C:1
class C(E):    attr = 1      #     \    /
class A(B, C): pass          #       A
X = A()                      #       |
print(X.attr)                #       X

# DFLR = [X, A, B, D, C, E]
# MRO  = [X, A, B, D, C, E, object]
# Prints "3" in both 3.X and 2.X (always)
```

Example: diamonds

```
class D:      attr = 3       #    D:3   D:3
class B(D):   pass           #    |     |
class C(D):   attr = 1       #    B     C:1
class A(B, C): pass          #     \   /
X = A()                      #       A
print(X.attr)                #       |
                             #       X

# DFLR = [X, A, B, D, C, D]
# MRO  = [X, A, B, C, D, object] (keeps last D only)
# Prints "1" in 3.X, "3" in 2.X ("1" if D(object))
```

New-style inheritance algorithm

Depending on class code, new-style inheritance may involve descriptors, metaclasses, and MROs as follows (name sources in this procedure are attempted in order, either as numbered or per their left-to-right order in "or" conjunctions).

To look up an attribute name:

1. From an *instance* I, search the instance, its class, and its superclasses, as follows:

   a. Search the __dict__ of all classes on the __mro__ found at I's __class__.

   b. If a data descriptor was found in step *a*, call its __get__() and exit.

   c. Else, return a value in the __dict__ of the instance I.

   d. Else, call a nondata descriptor or return a value found in step *a*.

2. From a *class* C, search the class, its superclasses, and its metaclasses tree, as follows:

   a. Search the __dict__ of all metaclasses on the __mro__ found at C's __class__.

b. If a data descriptor was found in step *a*, call its __get__() and exit.

c. Else, call a descriptor or return a value in the __dict__ of a class on *C*'s own __mro__.

d. Else, call a nondata descriptor or return a value found in step *a*.

3. In both rule 1 and 2, *built-in* operations (e.g., expressions) essentially use just step *a* sources for their implicit lookup of method names, and super() lookup is customized.

In addition, method __getattr__() may be run if defined when an attribute is not found; method __getattribute__() may be run for every attribute fetch; and the implied object superclass provides some defaults at the top of every class and metaclass tree (that is, at the end of every MRO).

As *special cases*, built-in operations skip name sources as described in rule 3, and the super() built-in function precludes normal inheritance. For objects returned by super(), attributes are resolved by a special context-sensitive scan of a limited portion of a class's MRO only, choosing the first descriptor or value found along the way, instead of running full inheritance (which is used on the super object itself only if this scan fails); see super() in "Built-in Functions".

To assign an attribute name:

A subset of the lookup procedure is run for attribute assignments:

- When applied to an *instance*, such assignments essentially follow steps *a* through *c* of rule 1, searching the instance's class tree, although step *b* calls __set__() instead of __get__(), and step *c* stops and stores in the instance instead of attempting a fetch.

- When applied to a *class*, such assignments run the same procedure on the class's metaclass tree: roughly the same as rule 2, but step *c* stops and stores in the class.

The __setattr__() method still catches all attribute assignments as before, although it becomes less useful for this method to use the instance __dict__ to assign names, as some new-style extensions such as slots, properties, and descriptors implement attributes at the class level—a sort of "virtual" instance data mechanism. Some instances might not have a __dict__ at all when slots are used (an optimization).

New-style precedence and context

New-style inheritance procedures effectively impose precedence rules on the foundational operation of name resolution, which may be thought of as follows (with corresponding steps of the inheritance algorithm in parentheses):

For instances, try:

1. Class-tree data descriptors (*1b*)

2. Instance-object values (*1c*)

3. Class-tree nondata descriptors (*1d*)

4. Class-tree values (*1d*)

For classes, try:

1. Metaclass-tree data descriptors (*2b*)

2. Class-tree descriptors (*2c*)

3. Class-tree values (*2c*)

4. Metaclass-tree nondata descriptors (*2d*)

5. Metaclass-tree values (*2d*)

Python runs at most one (for instances) or two (for classes) tree searches per name lookup, despite the presence of four or five name sources. See also the preceding section's description of the special case lookup procedure run for objects returned by the new-style super() built-in function.

See also "Methods for Descriptors" and "Metaclasses" for their subjects; "Operator Overloading Methods" for usage details of __setattr__(), __getattr__(), and __getattribute__(); and Python's *object.c* and *typeobject.c* source code files, which host the implementations of instances and classes, respectively (in Python's source code distribution).

Operator Overloading Methods

Classes may intercept and implement built-in operations by providing specially named method functions, all of which start and end with two underscores. These names are not reserved and can be inherited from superclasses as usual. Python locates and automatically calls at most one per operation.

Python calls a class's overloading methods when instances appear in expressions and other contexts. For example, if a class defines a method named __getitem__, and *X* is an instance of this class, the expression *X*[*i*] is equivalent to the method call *X*.__getitem__(*i*) (although, at present, using the method call form directly generally offers no speed advantage, and may even incur a penalty).

Overloading method names are somewhat arbitrary: a class's __add__ method need not perform an addition or concatenation (although it normally should serve a similar role). Moreover, classes generally can mix numeric and collection methods and mutable and immutable operations. Most operator overloading names have no defaults (except those in object for new-style classes), and running an operation raises an exception if its corresponding method is not defined (e.g., + without __add__).

The following subsections enumerate available operation methods. In this section, trailing parentheses are normally omitted from __*X*__ method names for brevity, as their context is implied. This section focuses on Python 3.X but gives operator overloading details common to most Python versions. See "Python 2.X Operator Overloading Methods" at the end of this section for items unique to Python lines.

Methods for All Types

__new__(*cls* [, *arg*]*)

Called to create and return a new instance of class *cls*. Receives constructor arguments *arg* passed to the class *cls*. If this returns an instance of the *cls* class, the instance's __init__ method is then invoked with the new *self* instance, plus the same constructor arguments; else __init__ is not run. Typically coded to call a superclass's __new__ via explicit superclass name or super() (see "Built-in Functions"), and manage and return the resulting instance. This is an automatically static method.

Not used in normal classes; intended to allow subclasses of immutable types to customize instance creation, and to allow custom *metaclasses* to tailor class creation. See also type() in "Built-in Functions" for the latter use case that invokes this method with class-creation arguments.

__init__(*self* [, *arg*]*)

Invoked on *class*(*args*...). This is the *constructor* method that initializes the new instance, *self*. When run for calls to a class name, *self* is provided automatically; *arg* is the arguments passed to the class name, and may be any function-definition argument form (see "The Expression Statement" and "The def Statement", including Table 14).

Although technically called after __new__, __init__ is the preferred way to configure new objects in all application-level classes. Must return no value, and if needed must call a superclass's __init__ manually passing along the instance to *self*, via explicit superclass name or super() (see "Built-in Functions"). Python calls just one __init__ automatically.

__del__(*self*)

Invoked on instance garbage collection. This is the *destructor* method that cleans up when an instance *self* is freed (reclaimed). Embedded objects are automatically freed when their container is (unless referenced from elsewhere). Exceptions during this method's run are ignored and simply print messages to sys.stderr. Hint: the try/finally statement allows more predictable termination actions for a code block; the with statement provides similar utility for supported object types.

__repr__(*self*)

Invoked on repr(*self*), interactive echoes, and nested appearances (as well as `self` in Python 2.X only). Also invoked on str(*self*) and print(*self*) if there is no __str__. This method generally returns a low-level "as code" string representation of *self*.

__str__(*self*)

Invoked on str(*self*) and print(*self*) (or uses __repr__ as a backup if defined). This method generally returns a high-level "user friendly" string representation of *self*.

__format__(*self, formatspec*)

Called by the format() built-in function—and by extension, the str.format() method of str strings—to produce a "formatted" string representation of the *self* object, per the *formatspec* string whose syntax for built-in types is as given for the same-named component in str.format(). See "Formatting method syntax", "String formatting method" and "Built-in Functions". New as of Python 2.6 and 3.0.

__bytes__(*self*)

Called by bytes() to return a bytes string representation of *self*, in Python 3.X only.

__hash__(*self*)

Invoked on dictionary[*self*] and hash(*self*), and other hashed collection operations, including those of the set object type. This method returns a unique and unchanging integer hash key, and interacts subtly with __eq__, both of which have defaults that ensure that all objects compare unequal except with themselves; see Python's manuals for more details.

__bool__(*self*)

Called for truth value testing and the built-in bool() function; returns False or True. When __bool__ is not defined, __len__() is called if it is defined and designates a true value with a nonzero length. If a class defines neither __len__ nor __bool__, all its instances are considered true. New in Python 3.X; in Python 2.X, this method is named __non zero__ instead of __bool__, but works the same way.

__call__(*self* [, *arg*]*)

Invoked on *self*(*args*...), when an instance is called like a function. *arg* may take any function-definition argument form. For example, the following two definitions:

```python
def __call__(self, a, b, c, d=5):
def __call__(self, *pargs, **kargs):
```

both match the following two calls:

```python
self(1, 2, 3, 4)
self(1, *(2,), c=3, **dict(d=4))
```

See "The def Statement", including Table 14, for more on *arg* options.

__getattr__(*self*, *name*)

Invoked on *self*.*name*, when *name* is an undefined attribute access (this method is not called if *name* exists in or is inherited by *self*). *name* is a string. This method returns an object or raises AttributeError.

Available in both classic and new-style classes. In both Python 3.X and new-style classes in 2.X, this is not run for __*X*__ attributes implicitly fetched by *built-in operations* (e.g., expressions); redefine such names in wrapper/proxy classes or superclasses. See also __dir__ in this list.

__setattr__(*self*, *name*, *value*)

Invoked on *self*.*name*=*value* (all attribute assignments). Hint: assign through __dict__ key or a superclass (e.g., object) to avoid recursive loops; a *self*.*attr*=*x* statement within a __setattr__ calls __setattr__ again, but a *self*.__dict__['*attr*']=x does not.

Recursion may also be avoided by calling a new-style class's object superclass version explicitly: object.__setattr__ (*self*, *attr*, *value*). This may be preferred or required in class trees that implement "virtual" instance attributes at the class level such as *slots*, *properties*, or *descriptors* (e.g., slots may preclude an instance __dict__).

__delattr__(*self*, *name*)
Invoked on del *self*.*name* (all attribute deletions). Hint: this must avoid recursive loops by routing attribute deletions through __dict__ or a superclass, much like __setattr__.

__getattribute__(*self*, *name*)
Called unconditionally to implement attribute accesses for instances of the class. If the class also defines __getattr__, it will never be called (unless it is called explicitly). This method should return the (computed) attribute value or raise an AttributeError exception. To avoid infinite recursion in this method, its implementation should always call the superclass method with the same name to access any attributes it needs (e.g., object.__getattribute__(*self*, *name*).

Available in Python 3.X, and in 2.X for *new-style* classes only. In both, this is not run for __*X*__ attributes implicitly fetched by *built-in operations* (e.g., expressions); redefine such names in wrapper/proxy classes. See also __dir__ in this list.

__lt__(*self*, *other*)
__le__(*self*, *other*)
__eq__(*self*, *other*)
__ne__(*self*, *other*)
__gt__(*self*, *other*)
__ge__(*self*, *other*)
Respectively, used on *self* < *other*, *self* <= *other*, *self* == *other*, *self* != *other*, *self* > *other*, and *self* >= *other*. Added in version 2.1, these are known as *rich comparison* methods

and are called for all comparison expressions in Python 3.X. For example, X < Y calls X.__lt__(Y) if defined. In Python 2.X only, these methods are called in preference to __cmp__, and __ne__ is also run for 2.X's *self <> other*.

These methods can *return* any value, but if the comparison operator is used in a Boolean context, the return value is interpreted as a Boolean result for the operator. These methods can also return (not raise) the special object NotImplemented if their operation is not supported for the operands (which works as though the method were not defined at all, and which forces Python 2.X to revert to the general __cmp__ method if defined).

There are no implied relationships among comparison operators. For example, X == Y being true does not imply that X != Y is false: __ne__ should be defined along with __eq__ if the operators are expected to behave symmetrically. There are also no right-side (swapped-argument) versions of these methods to be used when the left argument does not support the operation but the right argument does. __lt__ and __gt__ are each other's reflection, __le__ and __ge__ are each other's reflection, and __eq__ and __ne__ are their own reflections. Use __lt__ for sorting in Python 3.X, and see __hash__ in Python manuals for the role of __eq__ in hashing.

__slots__
> This class attribute can be assigned a string, sequence, or other iterable of strings giving the names of attributes of instances of the class. If defined in a *new-style* class (including all classes in Python 3.X), __slots__ generates a class-level management descriptor (see "Methods for Descriptors"); reserves space for the declared attributes in instances; and prevents the automatic creation of __dict__ for each instance (unless string '__dict__' is included in __slots__, in which case instances also have a __dict__ and attributes not named in __slots__ may be added dynamically).

Because they may suppress a __dict__ per instance, slots can optimize space usage. However, they are generally discouraged unless clearly warranted in pathological cases, due both to their potential to break some types of code, and their complex usage constraints (see Python manuals for details).

To support classes with __slots__, tools that generically list attributes or access them by string name must generally use storage-neutral tools such as the getattr(), setattr(), and dir(), which apply to both __dict__ and __slots__ attribute storage.

__instancecheck__(*self, instance*)
> Return true for isinstance() if *instance* is considered a direct or indirect instance of class. New in Python 3.X and 2.6; see Python manuals for usage.

__subclasscheck__(*self, subclass*)
> Return true for issubclass() if *subclass* should be considered a direct or indirect subclass of class. New in Python 3.X and 2.6; see Python manuals for usage.

__dir__(*self*)
> Called on dir(*self*) (see "Built-in Functions"). Returns a sequence of attribute names. Allows some classes to make their attributes known to introspection using dir(), when those attributes are computed dynamically with tools like __getattr__ but are known to the class itself. Dynamic use cases may not qualify directly, but some *general proxies* may be able to delegate this call to proxied objects to support attribute tools. New in Python 3.X; also backported for use in Python 2.6 and 2.7.

Methods for Collections (Sequences, Mappings)

__len__(*self*)
> Invoked on len(*self*) and possibly for truth-value tests. This method returns a collection's size. For Boolean tests, Python looks for __bool__ first, then __len__, and then

considers the object true (__bool__ is named __nonzero__ in Python 2.X). Zero length means false.

__contains__(*self*, *item*)

Invoked on *item* in *self* for custom membership tests (otherwise, membership uses __iter__, if defined, or else __getitem__). This method returns a true or false result.

__iter__(*self*)

Invoked on iter(*self*). Added in version 2.2, this method is part of the *iteration protocol*. It returns an object with a __next__ method (possibly *self*). The result object's __next__() method is then called repeatedly in all iteration contexts (e.g., for loops), and should return the next result or raise StopIteration to terminate the results progression.

If no __iter__ is defined, iteration falls back on __get item__. A class __iter__ method may also be coded with an embedded yield to return a generator with an automatically created __next__. In Python 2.X, __next__ is named next. See also "The for Statement", and "The iteration protocol".

__next__(*self*)

Invoked by the next(*self*) built-in function, and by all iteration contexts to advance through results. This method is part of the *iteration protocol*; see __iter__ in this list for more usage details. New in Python 3.X; in Python 2.X, this method is named next, but works the same way.

__getitem__(*self*, *key*)

Invoked on *self*[*key*], *self*[*i:j:k*], *x* in *self*, and possibly all iteration contexts. This method implements all indexing-related operations, including those for sequences and mappings. Iteration contexts (e.g., in and for) repeatedly index from 0 until IndexError, unless the preferred __iter__ is defined. __getitem__ and __len__ constitute *sequence protocol*.

In Python 3.X, this and the following two methods are also called for *slice* operations, in which case *key* is a slice object. Slice objects may be propagated to another slice expression, and have attributes start, stop, and step, any of which can be None (for absent). See also slice() in "Built-in Functions".

__setitem__(*self, key, value*)
> Invoked on *self*[*key*]=*value*, *self*[*i*:*j*:*k*]=*value*. This method is called for assignment to a collection key or index, or to a sequence's slice.

__delitem__(*self, key*)
> Invoked on del *self*[*key*], del *self*[*i*:*j*:*k*]. This method called is for index/key and sequence slice deletion.

__reversed__(*self*)
> Called if defined by the reversed() built-in function to implement custom reverse iteration. Returns a new iterable object that iterates over all the objects in the container in reverse order. If no __reversed__ is defined, reversed() expects and uses sequence protocol (methods __len__ and __getitem__).

Methods for Numbers (Binary Operators)

Numeric (and comparison) methods that do not support their operation for the supplied arguments should return (not raise) the special built-in NotImplemented object, which works as though the method were not defined at all. Operations not supported for any operand types should be left undefined.

See Table 1 for example roles of operators in built-in types, although operator meaning is defined by overloading classes. For example, __add__ is invoked on + for both numeric addition and sequence concatenation, but may have arbitrary semantics in new classes.

Basic binary methods

__add__(*self*, *other*)
    Invoked on *self* + *other*.

__sub__(*self*, *other*)
    Invoked on *self* - *other*.

__mul__(*self*, *other*)
    Invoked on *self* * *other*.

__truediv__(*self*, *other*)
    Invoked on *self* / *other* in Python 3.X. In Python 2.X, /
    instead invokes __div__ unless true division is enabled (see
    "Operator Usage Notes").

__floordiv__(*self*, *other*)
    Invoked on *self* // *other*.

__mod__(*self*, *other*)
    Invoked on *self* % *other*.

__divmod__(*self*, *other*)
    Invoked on divmod(*self*, *other*).

__pow__(*self*, *other* [, *modulo*])
    Invoked on pow(*self*, *other* [, *modulo*]) and *self* ** *other*.

__lshift__(*self*, *other*)
    Invoked on *self* << *other*.

__rshift__(*self*, *other*)
    Invoked on *self* >> *other*.

__and__(*self*, *other*)
    Invoked on *self* & *other*.

__xor__(*self*, *other*)
    Invoked on *self* ^ *other*.

__or__(*self*, *other*)
    Invoked on *self* | *other*.

Right-side binary methods

```
__radd__(self, other)
__rsub__(self, other)
__rmul__(self, other)
__rtruediv__(self, other)
__rfloordiv__(self, other)
__rmod__(self, other)
__rdivmod__(self, other)
__rpow__(self, other)
__rlshift__(self, other)
__rrshift__(self, other)
__rand__(self, other)
__rxor__(self, other)
__ror__(self, other)
```

These are right-side counterparts to the binary operators of the preceding section. Binary operator methods have a right-side variant that starts with an r prefix (e.g., __add__ and __radd__). Right-side variants have the same argument lists, but *self* is on the right side of the operator. For instance, *self* + *other* calls *self*.__add__(*other*), but *other* + *self* invokes *self*.__radd__(*other*).

The r right-side method is called only when the instance is on the right and the left operand is not an instance of a class that implements the operation:

- *instance* + *noninstance* runs __add__

- *instance* + *instance* runs __add__

- *noninstance* + *instance* runs __radd__

If two different class instances that overload the operation appear, the class on the left is preferred. __radd__ often converts or swaps order and re-adds to trigger __add__.

Augmented binary methods

```
__iadd__(self, other)
__isub__(self, other)
__imul__(self, other)
__itruediv__(self, other)
__ifloordiv__(self, other)
__imod__(self, other)
__ipow__(self, other[, modulo])
__ilshift__(self, other)
__irshift__(self, other)
__iand__(self, other)
__ixor__(self, other)
__ior__(self, other)
```

These are augmented assignment (in-place) methods. Respectively, they are called for the following assignment statement formats: +=, -=, *=, /=, //=, %=, **=, <<=, >>=, &=, ^=, and |=. These methods should attempt to do the operation in-place (modifying *self*) and return the result (which can be *self*). If a method is not defined, the augmented operation falls back on the normal methods. To evaluate *X* += *Y*, where *X* is an instance of a class that has an __iadd__, *X*.__iadd__(*Y*) is called. Otherwise, __add__ and __radd__ are considered.

Methods for Numbers (Other Operations)

```
__neg__(self)
```
Invoked on -*self*.

```
__pos__(self)
```
Invoked on +*self*.

```
__abs__(self)
```
Invoked on abs(*self*).

```
__invert__(self)
```
Invoked on ˜*self*.

__complex__(*self*)
    Invoked on complex(*self*).

__int__(*self*)
    Invoked on int(*self*).

__float__(*self*)
    Invoked on float(*self*).

__round__(*self*[, *n*])
    Invoked on round(*self*[, *n*]). New in Python 3.X.

__index__(*self*)
    Called to implement operator.index(). Also called in other contexts where Python requires an integer object. This includes instance appearances as indexes, as slice bounds, and as arguments to the built-in bin(), hex(), and oct() functions. Must return an integer.

    Similar in Python 3.X and 2.X, but not called for hex() and oct() in 2.X (these require __hex__ and __oct__ methods in 2.X). In Python 3.X, __index__ subsumes and replaces the __oct__ and __hex__ methods of Python 2.X, and the returned integer is formatted automatically.

Methods for Descriptors

The following methods apply only when an instance of a class defining them (a *descriptor* class) is assigned to a class attribute of another class (known as the *owner* class). These methods in the descriptor are then automatically invoked for access to the attribute in the owner class and its instances:

__get__(*self*, *instance*, *owner*)
    Called to get the attribute of the owner class or of an instance of that class. *owner* is always the owner class; *instance* is the instance the attribute was accessed through, or None when the attribute is accessed through the owner class directly; *self* is the instance of the descriptor class. Return the attribute value or raise AttributeError. Both *self* and *instance* may have state information.

__set__(*self, instance, value*)
> Called to set the attribute on an *instance* of the owner class to a new *value*.

__delete__(*self, instance*)
> Called to delete the attribute on an *instance* of the owner class.

Descriptors and their methods are available for *new-style* classes, including all classes in 3.X. They are fully operational in 2.X only if both the descriptor and owner classes are new-style. A descriptor with a __set__ is known as *data descriptor*, and is given precedence over other names in inheritance (see "Formal Inheritance Rules").

NOTE

The class "descriptors" here are distinct from "file descriptors" (see "Files" and "File Descriptor Tools" for the latter).

Methods for Context Managers

The following methods implement the context manager protocol, used by the with statement (see also "The with Statement" for the mechanism that uses these methods):

__enter__(*self*)
> Enter the runtime context related to this object. The with statement assigns this method's return value to the target specified in the as clause of the statement (if any).

__exit__(*self, type, value, traceback*)
> Exit the runtime context related to this object. The parameters after *self* describe the exception that caused the context to be exited. If the context exited without an exception, all three arguments are None. Otherwise, arguments are the same as sys.exc_info() results (see "The sys Module").

Return a true value to prevent a raised exception from being propagated by the caller.

Python 2.X Operator Overloading Methods

The preceding section notes semantic differences between operator overloading methods that are available in *both* Python 3.X and 2.X. This section notes content differences in the two lines.

Some of the methods described in the previous section work in 2.X for *new-style classes* only, which are an optional extension in the 2.X line. This includes __getattribute__, __slots__, and descriptor methods. Other methods may behave differently in 2.X for new-style classes (e.g., __getattr__ for built-ins), and some methods are available in later 2.X releases only (e.g., __dir__, __instancecheck__, __subclasscheck__). The following gives methods unique to each line.

Methods in Python 3.X only

The following methods are supported in Python 3.X but not Python 2.X:

- __round__

- __bytes__

- __bool__ (use method name __nonzero__ in Python 2.X, or __len__)

- __next__ (use method name next in Python 2.X)

- __truediv__ (available in Python 2.X only if true division is enabled: see "Operator Usage Notes")

- __index__ for oct(), hex() usage (use __oct__, __hex__ in Python 2.X)

Methods in Python 2.X only

The following methods are supported in Python 2.X but not Python 3.X:

__cmp__(*self, other*) *(and __rcmp__)*

Invoked on *self > other*, *other == self*, cmp(*self, other*), etc. This method is called for all comparisons for which no more specific method (such as __lt__) is defined or inherited. It returns –1, 0, or 1 for *self* less than, equal to, or greater than *other*. If no rich comparison or __cmp__ methods are defined, class instances compare by their identity (address in memory). The __rcmp__ right-side method is no longer supported as of version 2.1.

In Python 3.X, use the more specific comparison methods described earlier: __lt__, __ge__, __eq__, etc. Use __lt__ for sorting in Python 3.X.

__nonzero__(*self*)

Invoked on truth-value (otherwise, uses __len__ if defined).

In Python 3.X, this method is renamed __bool__.

__getslice__(*self, low, high*)

Invoked on *self*[*low:high*] for sequence slicing. If no __getslice__ is found, and for extended three-item slices, a *slice object* is created and passed to the __getitem__ method instead.

In Python 2.X, this and the next two methods are considered deprecated but are still supported—they are called for slice expressions if defined, in preference to their item-based counterparts. In Python 3.X, these three methods are removed entirely—slices always invoke __getitem__, __setitem__, or __delitem__ instead, with a slice object as its argument. See slice() in "Built-in Functions".

__setslice__(*self, low, high, value*)

Invoked on *self*[*low:high*]=*value* for sequence slice assignment. See also __getitem__ deprecation note earlier.

__delslice__(self, low, high)

Invoked on del self[low:high] for sequence slice deletion. See also __getitem__ deprecation note earlier.

__div__(self, other) (plus __rdiv__, __idiv__)

Invoked on self / other, unless true division is enabled (in which case __truediv__ is run instead). In Python 3.X, these are always subsumed by __truediv__, __rtruediv__, and __itruediv__ because / is always true division. See also "Operator Usage Notes". Hint: assign __truediv__ = __div__ to support both models in one method.

__long__(self)

Invoked on long(self). In Python 3.X, the int type subsumes the long type completely, so this method is removed.

__oct__(self)

Invoked on oct(self). This method returns an octal string representation. In Python 3.X, return an integer for __index__() instead.

__hex__(self)

Invoked on hex(self). This method returns a hex string representation. In Python 3.X, return an integer for __index__() instead.

__coerce__(self, other)

Invoked on the mixed-mode arithmetic expression, coerce(). This method returns a tuple of (self, other) converted to a common type. If __coerce__ is defined, it is generally called before any real operator methods are tried (e.g., before __add__). It should return a tuple containing operands converted to a common type (or None if it can't convert). See the Python Language Reference for more on coercion rules.

__unicode__(self)

Called by 2.X on unicode(self) to return a Unicode string for self (see "Python 2.X Built-in Functions"). This is the Unicode equivalent of __str__.

`__metaclass__`
    Class attribute assigned to the class's metaclass. In Python
    3.X, use instead `metaclass=M` keyword argument syntax in
    the class header line (see "Metaclasses").

Built-in Functions

All built-in names (functions, exceptions, and so on) exist in
the implied outer built-in scope, which corresponds to the
`builtins` module (named `__builtin__` in Python 2.X). Because
this scope is always searched last on name lookups, these functions are always available in programs without imports. However,
their names are not reserved words and might be hidden (shad-
owed) by assignments to the same name in global or local scopes.
Run `help(function)` for extra details on any call here.

This section focuses on Python 3.X but gives built-in function
details common to most Python versions. See "Python 2.X Built-
in Functions" at the end of this section for items unique to Python
lines:

`abs(N)`
    Returns the absolute value of a number *N*.

`all(iterable)`
    Returns `True` only if all elements of the *iterable* are true.

`any(iterable)`
    Returns `True` only if any element of the *iterable* is true.
    Hint: `filter(bool, I)` and `[x for x in I if x]` both collect
    all true values in an iterable *I*.

`ascii(object)`
    Like `repr()`, returns a string containing a printable repre-
    sentation of an object, but escapes the non-ASCII characters
    in the `repr()` result string using `\x`, `\u`, or `\U` escapes. This
    result is similar to that returned by `repr()` in Python 2.X.

bin(N)

Converts an integer number to a binary (base 2) digits string. The result is a valid Python expression. If argument N is not a Python int object, it must define an __index__() method that returns an integer. Hint: see also int(*string*, 2) to convert from binary, 0bNNN binary literals in code, and the b type code in str.format().

bool([X])

Returns the Boolean value of object X, using the standard truth testing procedure. If X is false or omitted, this returns False; otherwise, it returns True. bool is also a class, which is a subclass of int. The class bool cannot be subclassed further. Its only instances are False and True.

bytearray([arg [, encoding [, errors]]])

Returns a new array of bytes. The bytearray type is a mutable sequence of small integers in the range 0...255, which prints as ASCII text when possible. It is essentially a mutable variant of bytes, which supports most operations of mutable sequences, as well as most methods of the str string type. *arg* may be a str string with encoding name (and optionally errors) as in str() (described later in this list); an integer size to initialize an array of NULL (zero value) bytes; an iterable of small integers used to initialize the array such as a bytes string or another bytearray; an object conforming to the memory-view (previously known as buffer) interface used to initialize the array; or absent, to create a zero-length array. See also "byte and bytearray strings".

bytes([arg [, encoding [, errors]]])

Returns a new bytes object, which is an immutable sequence of integers in the range 0...255. bytes is an immutable version of bytearray. It has the same nonmutating string methods and sequence operations. It is commonly used to represent 8-bit byte strings of binary data (e.g., media, encoded Unicode text). Constructor arguments are interpreted as for bytearray(). bytes objects may also be created with the b'ccc' literal in Python 3.X (in 2.X, this makes a normal str). See also "byte and bytearray strings".

`callable(object)`

Returns True if *object* is callable; otherwise, returns False. This call is present in 2.X. In 3.X, it was removed in Python 3.0 and 3.1, but restored as of 3.2; in earlier 3.X, use `hasattr(object, '__call__')` instead.

`chr(I)`

Returns a one-character string whose Unicode code point is integer *I*. This is the inverse of ord() (e.g., chr(97) is 'a' and ord('a') is 97).

`classmethod(function)`

Returns a class method for a *function*. A class method receives the most specific (lowest) class of the subject instance as an implicit first argument, just like an instance method receives the instance. Useful for managing per-class data. Use the @classmethod function decorator form in version 2.4 and later (see "The def Statement").

`compile(string, filename, kind [, flags[, dont_inherit]])`

Compiles *string* into a code object. *string* is a Python string containing Python program code. *filename* is a string used in error messages (and is usually the name of the file from which the code was read, or '<string>' if typed interactively). *kind* can be 'exec' if *string* contains statements; 'eval' if *string* is an expression; or 'single', which prints the output of an expression statement that evaluates to something other than None. The resulting code object can be executed with exec() or eval() built-in function calls. The optional last two arguments control which future statements affect the string's compilation; if absent, the string is compiled with the future statements in effect at the place of the compile() call (see Python manuals for more details).

`complex([`*real* `[,` *imag*`]])`

> Builds a complex number object (this can also be coded using the J or j suffix: *real+imag*J). *imag* defaults to 0. If both arguments are omitted, returns 0j.

`delattr(`*object, name*`)`

> Deletes the attribute named *name* (a string) from *object*. Similar to del `object.name`, but *name* is a string, not a variable taken literally (e.g., `delattr(a, 'b')` is like del a.b).

`dict([`*mapping* `|` *iterable* `|` *keywords*`])`

> Returns a new dictionary initialized from a mapping; a sequence or other iterable of key/value pairs; or a set of keyword arguments. If no argument is given, it returns an empty dictionary. This is a subclassable type class name.

`dir([`*object*`])`

> If no argument is passed, this returns the list of names in the current local scope (namespace). When any *object* with attributes is passed as an argument, it returns the list of attribute names associated with that *object*. Works on modules, classes, and class instances, as well as built-in objects with attributes (lists, dictionaries, etc.). Its result includes inherited attributes, and is sorted; use __dict__ attributes for attribute lists of a single object only. This call runs a custom *object*. __dir__() if defined, which may provide names of computed attributes in dynamic or proxy classes.

`divmod(`*X, Y*`)`

> Returns a tuple of (*X / Y, X % Y*).

`enumerate(`*iterable, start*`=0)`

> Returns an iterable enumerate object. *iterable* must be a sequence or other iterable object that supports the iteration protocol. The __next__() method of the iterator returned by enumerate() returns a tuple containing a *count* (from start, or zero by default) and the corresponding *value* obtained from iterating over *iterable*. Useful for obtaining an indexed series of both positions and items, in iterations such as for loops (e.g., (0, x[0]), (1, x[1]), (2, x[2]), …).

Available in version 2.3 and later. See also "The enum Module" for fixed enumerations in Python 3.4.

`eval(expr [, globals [, locals]])`

Evaluates *expr*, which is assumed to be either a Python string containing a Python expression or a compiled code object. *expr* is evaluated in the namespace scopes of the *eval* call itself, unless the *globals* and/or *locals* namespace dictionary arguments are passed. *locals* defaults to *globals* if only *globals* is passed. This call returns the *expr* result. Also see the `compile()` function earlier in this section to precompile, and the `exec()` built-in, later in this section, to run statement strings. Hint: do not use this to evaluate untrustworthy code strings, as they run as program code.

`exec(stmts [, globals [, locals]])`

Evaluates *stmts*, which is assumed to be either a Python string containing Python statements or a compiled code object. If *stmts* is a string, the string is parsed as a suite of Python statements, which is then executed unless a syntax error occurs. If it is a code object, it is simply executed. *globals* and *locals* work the same as in `eval()`, and `compile()` may be used to precompile to code objects. This is available as a statement form in Python 2.X (see "Python 2.X Statements"), and has morphed between statement and function forms more than once in Python's history. Hint: do not use this to evaluate untrustworthy code strings, as they run as program code.

`filter(function, iterable)`

Returns those elements of *iterable* for which *function* returns a true value. *function* takes one parameter. If *function* is None, this returns all the true items in *iterable* —which is the same as passing the built-in bool to *function*.

In Python 2.X, this call returns a *list*. In Python 3.X, it returns an *iterable* object that generates values on demand and can be traversed only once (wrap in a `list()` call to force results generation if required).

`float([X])`

> Converts a number or a string *X* to a floating-point number (or 0.0 if no argument is passed). See also "Numbers" for example uses. This is a subclassable type class name.

`format(value [, formatspec])`

> Converts an object *value* to a formatted representation, as controlled by string *formatspec*. The interpretation of *formatspec* depends on the type of the *value* argument; a standard formatting syntax is used by most built-in types, described for the string formatting method earlier in this book (see *formatspec* in "Formatting method syntax"). `format(value, formatspec)` calls `value.__format__(formatspec)`, and is a base operation of the `str.format()` method (e.g., `format(1.3333, '.2f')` is equivalent to `'{0:.2f}'.format(1.3333)`).

`frozenset([iterable])`

> Returns a *frozen set* object whose elements are taken from *iterable*. Frozen sets are immutable sets that have no update methods, and may be nested in other sets.

`getattr(object, name [, default])`

> Returns the value of attribute *name* (a string) from *object*. Similar to *object.name*, but *name* evaluates to a string, and is not a variable name taken literally (e.g., `getattr(a, 'b')` is like a.b). If the named attribute does not exist, *default* is returned if provided; otherwise, `AttributeError` is raised.

`globals()`

> Returns a dictionary containing the caller's global variables (e.g., the enclosing module's names).

`hasattr(object, name)`

> Returns `True` if *object* has an attribute called *name* (a string); `False` otherwise.

hash(*object*)

Returns the hash value of *object* (if it has one). Hash values are integers used to quickly compare dictionary keys during a dictionary lookup. Invokes *object*.__hash__().

help([*object*])

Invokes the built-in help system. This function is intended for interactive use. If no argument is given, an interactive help session starts in the interpreter console. If the argument is a string, it is looked up as the name of a module, function, class, method, keyword, or documentation topic, and its help text is displayed. If the argument is any other kind of object, help for that object is generated (e.g., help(list.pop))

hex(*N*)

Converts an integer number *N* to a hexadecimal (base 16) digits string. If argument *N* is not a Python int object, in Python 3.X it must define an __index__() method that returns an integer (in 2.X, __hex__() is called instead).

id(*object*)

Returns the identity integer of *object*, which is unique for the calling process among all existing objects (i.e., its address in memory).

__import__(*name*, [...*other args*...])

Imports and returns a module, given its *name* as a string at runtime (e.g., mod = __import__('mymod')). This call is generally faster than constructing and executing an import statement string with exec(). This function is called by import and from statements internally and can be overridden to customize import operations. All arguments but the first have advanced roles; see the Python Library Reference. See also the standard library's imp module and importlib .import_module() call, as well as "The import Statement".

input([*prompt*])

Prints a *prompt* string if given, and then reads a line from the *stdin* input stream (sys.stdin) and returns it as a string. It strips the trailing \n at the end of the line and raises EOFError at the end of the *stdin* stream. On platforms where GNU readline is supported, input() uses it. In Python 2.X, this function is named raw_input().

int([*number* | *string* [, *base*]])

Converts a number or string to a plain integer. Conversion of floating-point numbers to integers truncates toward 0. *base* can be passed only if the first argument is a string, and defaults to 10. If *base* is passed as 0, the base is determined by the string's contents (as a code literal); otherwise, the value passed for *base* is used for the base of the conversion of the string. *base* may be 0, and 2...36. The string may be preceded by a sign and surrounded by ignored whitespace. If no arguments, returns 0. See also "Numbers" for example uses. This is a subclassable type class name.

isinstance(*object*, *classinfo*)

Returns True if *object* is an instance of *classinfo*, or an instance of any subclass thereof. *classinfo* can also be a tuple of classes and/or types. In Python 3.X, types are classes, so there is no special case for types. In Python 2.X, the second argument can also be a type object, making this function useful in both Pythons as an alternative type-testing tool (isinstance(*X*, *Type*) versus type(*X*) is *Type*).

issubclass(*class1*, *class2*)

Returns True if *class1* is derived from *class2*. *class2* can also be a tuple of classes.

iter(*object* [, *sentinel*])

Returns an iterator object that can be used to step through items in iterable *object*. Iterator objects returned have a __next__() method that returns the next item or raises StopIteration to end the progression. All iteration contexts in Python use this protocol to advance, if supported by *object*. The next(*I*) built-in function also calls *I*.__next__() automatically. If one argument, *object* is assumed to provide its own iterator or be a sequence; if two arguments, *object* is a callable that is called until it returns

sentinel. The iter() call can be overloaded in classes with
__iter__().

In Python 2.X, iterator objects have a method named next()
instead of __next__(). For forward and backward compatibility, the next() built-in function is also available in 2.X
(as of 2.6) and calls *I*.next() instead of *I*.__next__(). Prior
to 2.6, *I*.next() may be called explicitly instead. See also
next() in this list, and "The iteration protocol".

len(*object*)

Returns the number of items (length) in a collection
object, which may be a sequence, mapping, set, or other
(e.g., a user-defined collection).

list([*iterable*])

Returns a new list containing all the items in any *iterable*
object. If *iterable* is already a list, it returns a (shallow) copy
of it. If no arguments, returns a new empty list. This is a
subclassable type class name.

locals()

Returns a dictionary containing the local variables of the
caller (with one *key*: *value* entry per local).

map(*function, iterable* [, *iterable*]*)

Applies *function* to each item of any sequence or other
iterable object *iterable*, and returns the individual results.
For example, map(abs, (1, -2)) returns 1 and 2. If additional iterable arguments are passed, *function* must take
that many arguments, and is passed one item from each
iterable on every call; in this mode, iteration stops at the
end of the shortest iterable.

In Python 2.X, this returns a *list* of the individual call results.
In Python 3.X, it instead returns an *iterable* object that generates results on demand and can be traversed only once
(wrap it in a list() call to force results generation if
required).

Also in Python 2.X (but not Python 3.X), if *function* is None, map() collects all the *iterable* items into a result list; for multiple iterables, the result combines their items in tuples, and all iterables are padded with Nones to the length of the longest. Similar utility is available in Python 3.X in standard library module itertools.

max(*iterable* [, *arg*]* [, key=*func*])

> With a single argument *iterable*, returns the highest-valued item of a nonempty iterable (e.g., string, tuple, list, set). With more than one argument, it returns the highest value among all the arguments. The optional keyword-only key argument specifies a one-argument value transform function like that used for list.sort() and sorted() (see "Lists" and "Built-in Functions").

memoryview(*object*)

> Returns a memory view object created from the given *object* argument. Memory views allow Python code to access the internal data of an object that supports the protocol without copying the object. Memory can be interpreted as simple bytes or more complex data structures. Built-in objects that support the memory-view protocol include bytes and bytearray. See Python manuals; memory views are largely a replacement for the Python 2.X buffer() protocol and built-in function, although memoryview() is backported to Python 2.7 for 3.X compatibility.

min(*iterable* [, *arg*]* [, key=*func*])

> With a single argument *iterable*, returns the lowest-valued item of a nonempty iterable (e.g., string, tuple, list, set). With more than one argument, it returns the lowest value among all the arguments. The key argument is as in max() (in this list).

next(*iterator* [, *default*])

> Retrieves the next item from the *iterator* object by calling its __next__() method (in 3.X). If the *iterator* is exhausted, *default* is returned if given; otherwise, StopIteration is raised. This function is also available in Python 2.6 and 2.7,

where it calls *iterator*.next() instead of *iterator*. __next__(). This aids 2.X forward compatibility with 3.X, and 3.X backward compatibility with 2.X. In Python 2.X prior to 2.6, this call is missing; use *iterator*.next() manually instead for manual iterations. See also iter() in this list, and "The iteration protocol".

object()

Returns a new featureless object. object (its literal name) is a superclass to all new-style classes, which includes all classes in Python 3.X, and classes explicitly derived from object in Python 2.X. It has a small set of default methods (see dir(object)).

oct(*N*)

Converts a number *N* to an octal (base 8) digits string. If argument *N* is not a Python int object, in Python 3.X it must define an __index__() method that returns an integer (in 2.X, __oct__() is called instead).

open(...)

```
open(file
   [, mode='r'
   [, buffering=-1
   [, encoding=None        # Text mode only
   [, errors=None          # Text mode only
   [, newline=None         # Text mode only
   [, closefd=True,        # Descriptors only
   [, opener=None  ]]]]]]]) # Custom opener 3.3+
```

Returns a new *file object* connected to the external file named by *file*, or raises IOError (or an OSError subclass as of 3.3) if the open fails. This section describes Python 3.X's open(); for Python 2.X usage, see "Python 2.X Built-in Functions".

file is usually a text or bytes string object giving the name (including its path if the file isn't in the current working directory) of the file to be opened. *file* may also be an integer file descriptor of the file to be wrapped. If a file descriptor is given, it is closed when the returned I/O object is closed, unless closefd is set to False. All the following options may be passed as keyword arguments.

mode is an optional string that specifies the mode in which the file is opened. It defaults to 'r', which means open for reading in text mode. Other common values are 'w' for writing (truncating the file if it already exists), and 'a' for appending. In text mode, if encoding is not specified, the encoding used is platform dependent, and newlines are translated to and from '\n' by default. For reading and writing raw bytes, use binary modes 'rb', 'wb', or 'ab', and leave encoding unspecified.

Available modes that may be combined: 'r' for read (default); 'w' for write, truncating the file first; 'a' for write, appending to the end of the file if it exists; 'b' for binary mode; 't' for text mode (default); '+' to open a disk file for updating (reading and writing); 'U' for universal newline mode (for backward compatibility only). The default 'r' mode is the same as 'rt' (open for reading text). For binary random access, the mode 'w+b' opens and truncates the file to zero bytes, while 'r+b' opens the file without truncation.

Python distinguishes between files opened in binary and text modes, even when the underlying operating system does not:

- For *input*, files opened in binary mode (by appending 'b' to mode) return contents as bytes objects without any Unicode decoding or line-end translations. In text mode (the default, or when 't' is appended to mode), the contents of the file are returned as str strings after the bytes are decoded using either an explicitly passed Unicode encoding name or a platform-dependent default, and line-ends are translated per newline.

- For *output*, binary mode expects a bytes or bytearray and writes it unchanged. Text mode expects a str, and encodes it per a Unicode encoding and applies line end translations per newline before writing.

`buffering` is an optional integer used to set buffering policy. By default (when not passed or value –1), full buffering is on. Pass 0 to switch buffering off (allowed in binary mode only); 1 to set line buffering (only in text mode); and an integer > 1 for full buffering and buffer size. Buffered data transfers might not be immediately fulfilled (use `file.flush()` to force buffers to be emptied).

`encoding` is the name of the encoding used to decode or encode a text file's content on transfers. This should be used in text mode only. The default encoding is platform dependent (obtained from `locale.getpreferredencoding()`), but any encoding supported by Python can be passed. See the `codecs` module in the Python standard library for the list of supported encodings.

`errors` is an optional string that specifies how to handle encoding errors. This should be used in text mode only. It may be passed `'strict'` (the default, for `None`) to raise a `ValueError` exception on encoding errors; `'ignore'` to ignore errors (but ignoring encoding errors can result in data loss); `'replace'` to use a replacement marker for invalid data; and more. See Python manuals and `codecs.register _error()` in Python's standard library for permitted error values, and `str()` in this list for related tools.

`newline` controls how universal newlines work, and applies to text mode only. It can be `None` (the default), `''`, `'\n'`, `'\r'`, and `'\r\n'`:

- On *input*, if newline is `None`, universal newlines mode is enabled: lines may end in `'\n'`, `'\r'`, or `'\r\n'`, and all these are translated to `'\n'` before being returned to the caller. If newline is `''`, universal newline mode is enabled, but line endings are returned to the caller untranslated. If it has any of the other legal values, input lines are terminated only by the given string, and the line ending is returned to the caller untranslated.

- On *output*, if newline is None, any '\n' characters written are translated to the system default line separator, os.linesep. If newline is ' ', no translation takes place. If it is any of the other legal values, any '\n' characters written are translated to the given string.

If closefd is False, the underlying file descriptor will be kept open when the file is closed. This does not work when a file name is given as a string and must be True (the default) in that case. If opener is passed a callable in Python 3.3 and later, a file descriptor is obtained by *opener*(file, *flags*), with arguments as for os.open() (see "The os System Module").

See also "Files" for the interface of objects returned by open(). Hint: any object that supports the file object's method interface can generally be used in contexts that expect a file (e.g., see *socketobj*.makefile(), Python 3.X's io.StringIO(*str*) and io.BytesIO(*bytes*), and Python 2.X's StringIO.stringIO(*str*), all in the Python standard library).

NOTE

Because file mode implies both configuration options and string datatypes in 3.X, it is useful to think of open() in terms of *two distinct flavors*—text and binary, as specified in the mode string. Python developers chose to overload a single function to support the two file types, with mode-specific arguments and differing content types, rather than provide two separate open() functions. The underlying io class library—to which open() is a frontend in 3.X—*does* specialize file object types for modes. See Python manuals for more on the io module. io is also available in 2.X as of 2.6 as an alternative to its built-in file type, but is the normal file interface for open() in 3.X.

`ord(C)`

>   Returns an integer code point value of a one-character string
>   C. For ASCII characters, this is the 7-bit ASCII code of C; in
>   general, this is the Unicode code point of a one-character
>   Unicode string C. See also this call's chr() inverse in this list.

`pow(X, Y[, Z])`

>   Returns X to power Y [modulo Z]. This is similar to the **
>   expression operator.

`print(...)`

```
print([object [, object]*]
      [, sep=' '] [, end='\n']
      [, file=sys.stdout] [, flush=False])
```

Prints optional *object*(s) to the stream file, separated by
sep, followed by end, with an optional post-printing forced
flush. The last four arguments, if present, must be given as
keyword arguments, and default as shown; flush is available
as of Python 3.3.

All nonkeyword arguments are converted to strings using
the equivalent of str(), and written to the stream. Both sep
and end must either be strings, or None (meaning use their
default values). If no *object* is given, end is written. file
must be an object with a write(*string*) method, but need
not be an actual file; if it is not passed or is None, sys.stdout
will be used.

Print functionality is available as a statement form in Python
2.X. See also "The print Statement".

`property([fget[, fset[, fdel[, doc]]]])`

>   Returns a property attribute for new-style classes (classes
>   that derive from object, including all in 3.X). *fget* is a func-
>   tion for getting an attribute value, *fset* is a function for set-
>   ting, and *fdel* is a function for deleting. This call may be
>   used as a function decorator itself (@property), and returns
>   an object with methods *getter*, *setter*, and *deleter*, which
>   may also be used as decorators in this role (see "The def

Statement"). Implemented with descriptors (see "Methods for Descriptors").

range([*start*,] *stop* [, *step*])

Returns successive integers between *start* and *stop*. With one argument, it returns integers from 0 through *stop*-1. With two arguments, it returns integers from *start* through *stop*-1. With three arguments, it returns integers from *start* through *stop*-1, adding *step* to each predecessor in the result. *start*, *step* default to 0, 1.

step may be > 1 to skip items (range(0, 20, 2) is a list of even integers from 0 through 18), or negative to count down from the *start* high value (range(5, -5, -1) is 5 through -4). This call is often used to generate offset lists or repeat counts in for loops and other iterations.

In Python 2.X, this call returns a *list*. In Python 3.X, it returns an *iterable* object that generates values on demand and can be traversed multiple times (wrap in a list() call to force results generation if required).

repr(*object*)

Returns the lower-level "as-code" printable string representation of object. The string generally takes a form potentially parseable by eval(), or gives more details than str() (in this list). In Python 2.X only, this is equivalent to `object` (the backquotes expression, removed in Python 3.X). See __repr__() in "Operator Overloading Methods".

reversed(*seq*)

Returns a reverse iterable. *seq* must be an object that has a __reversed__() method or supports the sequence protocol (the __len__() method, and the __getitem__() method called with integer arguments starting at 0).

round(*X* [, *N*])

Returns the floating-point value *X* rounded to *N* digits after the decimal point. *N* defaults to zero, and may be negative to denote digits to the left of the decimal point. The return value is an integer if called with one argument; otherwise, it is of the same type as *X*. In Python 2.X only, the result is always a floating-point. In Python 3.X only, this calls *X*.__round__().

set([*iterable*])

Returns a set whose elements are taken from *iterable*. The elements must be immutable. To represent sets of sets, the nested sets should be frozenset objects. If *iterable* is not specified, this returns a new empty set. Available since version 2.4. See also "Sets", and the {...} set literal in Python 3.X and 2.7.

setattr(*object*, *name*, *value*)

Assigns *value* to the attribute *name* (a string) in *object*. Similar to *object.name = value*, but *name* evaluates to a string, and is not a variable name taken literally (e.g., setattr(a, 'b', c) is equivalent to a.b = c).

slice([*start* ,] *stop* [, *step*])

Returns a slice object representing a range, with read-only attributes *start*, *stop*, and *step*, any of which can be None. Arguments are interpreted the same as for range(). Slice objects may be used in place of *i:j:k* slice notation (e.g., *X*[*i:j*] is equivalent to *X*[slice(*i*, *j*)]).

sorted(*iterable*, key=None, reverse=False)

Returns a new sorted list from the items in *iterable*. The optional keyword arguments key and reverse have the same meaning as those for the list.sort() method described in "Lists"; key is a one-argument value transform function. This works on any iterable and returns a new object instead of changing a list in-place, and is thus useful in for loops (and more) to avoid splitting sort calls out to separate statements due to None returns. Available in version 2.4 and later.

In Python 2.X, this has call signature sorted(*iterable*, cmp=None, key=None, reverse=False), where optional arguments cmp, key, and reverse have the same meaning as those for the Python 2.X list.sort() method described earlier in "Lists".

staticmethod(*function*)

> Returns a static method for *function*. A static method does not receive an instance as an implicit first argument, and so is useful for processing class attributes that span instances. Use the @staticmethod function decorator in version 2.4 and later (see "The def Statement"). In Python 3.X only, this built-in is not required for simple functions in classes called only through class objects (and never through instance objects).

str([*object* [, *encoding* [, *errors*]]])

> This call (which is also a subclassable type name) operates in one of two modes in Python 3.X determined by call pattern:

> - *Print string*: when only *object* is given, this returns the higher-level "user-friendly" printable string representation of *object*. For strings, this is the string itself. Unlike repr(*X*), str(*X*) does not always attempt to return a string that is acceptable to eval(); its goal is to return a readable and printable string. With no arguments, this returns the empty string. See also __str__() in "Operator Overloading Methods", invoked by this mode.

> - *Unicode decoding*: if *encoding* and/or *errors* are passed, this will decode the object, which can either be a byte string or a character buffer, using the codec for *encoding*. The *encoding* parameter is a string giving the name of a Unicode encoding; if the encoding is not known, LookupError is raised. Error handling is done according to *errors*, which may be 'strict' (the default), to raise ValueError on encoding errors; 'ignore', to silently ignore errors and potentially lose data; or 'replace', to replace input characters that cannot be decoded with the official Unicode replacement character, U+FFFD. See also the standard library's codecs module, and the similar bytes.decode()

method (e.g., `b'a\xe4'.decode('latin-1')` is equivalent to `str(b'a\xe4', 'latin-1')`).

In Python 2.X, this call has simpler signature `str([object])`, and returns a string containing the higher-level printable representation of *object* (equivalent to the first Python 3.X usage mode given in the preceding list's first bullet item). Unicode decoding is implemented in 2.X by string methods or the 2.X `unicode()` call, which is essentially the same as the 3.X `str()` here (see the next section).

`sum(iterable [, start])`

Sums *start* and all the items of any *iterable*, and returns the total. *start* defaults to 0. The iterable's items are normally numbers and are not allowed to be strings. Hint: to concatenate an iterable of strings, use `''.join(iterable)`.

`super([type [, object]])`

Returns the superclass of *type*. If the second argument is omitted, the super object returned is unbound. If the second argument is an object, `isinstance(object, type)` must be true. If the second argument is a type, `issubclass(object, type)` must be true. This call works for all classes in 3.X, but only for new-style classes in Python 2.X, where *type* is also not optional.

In 3.X only, calling `super()` without arguments in a class method is implicitly equivalent to `super(containing-class, method-self-argument)`. Whether implicit or explicit, this call form creates a bound proxy object that pairs the *self* instance with access to the calling class's location on the MRO of *self*'s class. This proxy object is usable for later superclass attribute references and method calls. See also "New-style classes: MRO" for more on MRO ordering.

Because `super()` always selects a *next* class on the MRO—the first class following the calling class having a requested attribute, whether it is a true superclass or not—it can be used for method call routing. In a *single-inheritance* class tree, this call may be used to refer to parent superclasses generically without naming them explicitly. In *multiple-inheritance* trees, this call can be used to implement cooperative method-call dispatch that propagates calls through a tree.

The latter usage mode, cooperative method-call dispatch, may be useful in diamonds, as a conforming method call chain visits each superclass just once. However, super() can also yield highly implicit behavior which for some programs may not invoke superclasses as expected or required. The super() method dispatch technique generally imposes three requirements:

- *Anchors*: the method called by super() must exist— which requires extra code if no call-chain anchor is present.

- *Arguments*: the method called by super() must have the same argument signature across the entire class tree—which can impair flexibility, especially for implementation-level methods like constructors.

- *Deployment*: every appearance of the method called by super() but the last must use super() itself—which can make it difficult to use existing code, change call ordering, override methods, and code self-contained classes.

Because of these constraints, calling superclass methods by explicit superclass name instead of using super() may in some cases be simpler, more predictable, or required. For a superclass S, the explicit and traditional form S.method(self) is equivalent to the implicit super().method(). See also "New-style inheritance algorithm" for more on the super() attribute lookup special case; instead of running full inheritance, its result objects scan a context-dependent tail portion of a class tree's MRO, selecting the first matching descriptor or value.

`tuple([`*`iterable`*`])`

> Returns a new tuple with the same elements as any *iterable* passed in. If *iterable* is already a tuple, it is returned directly (not a copy); this suffices because tuples are immutable. If no argument, returns a new empty tuple. This is also a subclassable type class name.

`type(`*`object`* `| (`*`name, bases, dict`*`))`

> This call (which is also a subclassable type name) is used in two different modes, determined by call pattern:
>
> - *With one argument*, returns a type object representing the type of *object*. Useful for type testing in `if` statements (e.g., `type(`*`X`*`)==type([])`). See also module `types` in the standard library for preset type objects that are not built-in names, and `isinstance()` earlier in this section. In new-style classes, `type(`*`object`*`)` is generally the same as *`object`*`.__class__`. In Python 2.X only, the `types` module also includes synonyms for most built-in type names.
>
> - *With three arguments*, serves as a constructor, returning a new type object. This is a dynamic form of the `class` statement. The *name* string is the class name and becomes the `__name__` attribute; the *bases* tuple itemizes the base (super) classes and becomes the `__bases__` attribute; and the *dict* dictionary is the namespace containing attribute definitions for the class body and becomes the `__dict__` attribute. For example, the following are equivalent:
>
>   ```
>   class X(object): a = 1
>   X = type('X', (object,), dict(a=1))
>   ```
>
>   This mapping is employed for *metaclass* construction, in which such `type()` calls are issued automatically, and generally invoke a metaclass's `__new__()` and/or `__init__()` with class creation arguments, for subclasses of `type`.

See also "Metaclasses", "Class decorators in Python 3.X, 2.6, and 2.7", and __new__() in "Operator Overloading Methods".

`vars([object])`

> Without arguments, returns a dictionary containing the current local scope's names. With a module, class, or class instance *object* as an argument, it returns a dictionary corresponding to *object*'s attribute namespace (i.e., its __dict__). The result should not be modified. Hint: useful for referring to variables in string formatting.

`zip([iterable [, iterable]*])`

> Returns a series of tuples, where each ith tuple contains the ith element from each of the argument iterables. For example, `zip('ab', 'cd')` returns ('a', 'c') and ('b', 'd'). At least one iterable is required, or the result is empty. The result series is truncated to the length of the shortest argument iterable. With a single iterable argument, it returns a series of one-tuples. May also be used to unzip zipped tuples: X, Y = zip(*zip(T1, T2)).

> In Python 2.X, this returns a *list*. In Python 3.X, it returns an *iterable* object that generates values on demand and can be traversed only once (wrap in a list() call to force results generation if required). In Python 2.X (but not Python 3.X), when there are multiple argument iterables of the same length, zip() is similar to map() with a first argument of None.

Python 2.X Built-in Functions

The preceding section notes semantic differences between built-in functions that are available in *both* Python 3.X and 2.X. This section notes content differences in the two lines.

Python 3.X built-ins not supported by Python 2.X

Python 2.X does not generally have the following Python 3.X built-in functions:

`ascii()`

> This works like Python 2.X's `repr()`.

`exec()`

> This is a statement form in Python 2.X with similar semantics.

`memoryview()`

> But made available in Python 2.7 for 3.X compatibility.

`print()`

> Present in Python 2.X's `__builtin__` module, but not directly usable syntactically without `__future__` imports, as printing is a statement form and reserved word in Python 2.X (see "The print Statement").

Python 2.X built-ins not supported by Python 3.X

Python 2.X has the following additional built-in functions, some of which are available in different forms in Python 3.X:

`apply(func, pargs [, kargs])`

> Calls any callable object *func* (a function, method, class, etc.), passing the positional arguments in tuple *pargs*, and the keyword arguments in dictionary *kargs*. It returns the *func* call result.
>
> In Python 3.X, this is removed. Use the argument-unpacking call syntax instead: `func(*pargs, **kargs)`. This starred form is also preferred in Python 2.X, both because it is more general and because it is symmetric with function definitions' starred terms (see "The Expression Statement").

`basestring()`

> The base (super) class for normal and Unicode strings (useful for `isinstance()` tests).
>
> In Python 3.X, the single `str` type represents all text (both 8-bit and richer Unicode).

`buffer(object [, offset [, size]])`

Returns a new buffer object for a conforming *object* (see the Python 2.X Library Reference).

This call is removed in Python 3.X. The new `memoryview()` built-in provides similar functionality in 3.X, and is also available in Python 2.7 for forward compatibility.

`cmp(X, Y)`

Returns a negative integer, zero, or a positive integer to designate *X < Y*, *X == Y*, or *X > Y*, respectively.

In Python 3.X, this is removed, but may be simulated as: `(X > Y) - (X < Y)`. However, most common `cmp()` use cases (comparison functions in sorts, and the `__cmp__()` method of classes) have also been removed in Python 3.X.

`coerce(X, Y)`

Returns a tuple containing the two numeric arguments *X* and *Y* converted to a common type.

This call is removed in Python 3.X. (Its main use case was for Python 2.X classic classes.)

`execfile(filename [, globals [, locals]])`

Like `eval()`, but runs all the code in a file whose string name is passed in as *filename* (instead of an expression). Unlike imports, this does not create a new module object for the file. It returns `None`. Namespaces for code in *filename* are as for `eval()`.

In Python 3.X, this may be simulated as: `exec(open (filename).read())`.

`file(filename [, mode [, bufsize]])`

An alias for the `open()` built-in function, and the subclassable class name of the built-in file type.

In Python 3.X, the name `file` is removed: use `open()` to access files, and the `io` standard library module to customize them (`io` is used by `open()` in 3.X, and is an option in 2.X as of 2.6).

`input([prompt])` *(original 2.X form)*

Prints *prompt*, if given. Then it reads an input line from the *stdin* stream (`sys.stdin`), evaluates it as Python code, and returns the result. In 2.X, this is like `eval(raw_input(prompt))`. Hint: do not use this to evaluate untrustworthy code strings, as they run as program code.

In Python 3.X, because `raw_input()` was renamed `input()`, the original Python 2.X `input()` is no longer available, but may be simulated as: `eval(input(prompt))`.

`intern(string)`

Enters *string* in the table of "interned strings" and returns the interned string. Interned strings are "immortals" and serve as a performance optimization. (They can be compared by fast `is` identity, rather than `==` equality.)

In Python 3.X, this call has been moved to `sys.intern()`. Import module `sys` to use it, and see "The sys Module" for more details.

`long(X [, base])`

Converts a number or a string *X* to a long integer. *base* can be passed only if *X* is a string. If 0, the base is determined by the string contents; otherwise, it is used for the base of the conversion. This is a subclassable type class name.

In Python 3.X, the `int` integer type supports arbitrarily long precision, and so subsumes Python 2.X's `long` type. Use `int()` in Python 3.X.

`raw_input([prompt])`

This is the Python 2.X name of the Python 3.X `input()` function described in the preceding section: prints *prompt*, reads and returns, but does not evaluate, the next input line.

In Python 3.X, use the `input()` built-in.

`reduce(func, iterable [, init])`

Applies the two-argument function *func* to successive items from *iterable*, so as to reduce the collection to a single value. If *init* is given, it is prepended to *iterable*.

In Python 3.X, this built-in is still available, as `functools.reduce()`. Import module `functools` to use it.

`reload(module)`

Reloads, reparses, and reexecutes an already imported *module* in the module's current namespace. Reexecution replaces prior values of the module's attributes in-place. *module* must reference an existing module object; it is not a new name or a string. This is useful in interactive mode if you want to reload a module after fixing it, without restarting Python. It returns the *module* object. See also the `sys.modules` table, where imported modules are retained (and can be deleted to force reimports).

In Python 3.X, this built-in is still available as `imp.reload()`. Import module `imp` to use it.

`unichr(I)`

Returns the Unicode string of one character whose Unicode code point is integer *I* (e.g., `unichr(97)` returns string `u'a'`). This is the inverse of `ord()` for Unicode strings, and the Unicode version of `chr()`. The argument must be in range 0...65,535 inclusive, or `ValueError` is raised.

In Python 3.X, normal strings represent Unicode characters: use the `chr()` call instead (e.g., `ord('\xe4')` is 228, and `chr(228)` and `chr(0xe4)` both return `'ä'`).

`unicode([object [, encoding [, errors]]])`

Works similarly to the 3.X `str()` function (see `str()` in the preceding section for more details). With just *one* argument, this returns a high-level print string representation for *object*, but as a 2.X Unicode string (not a *str*). With *more than one* argument, this performs Unicode decoding of string *object* using the codec for *encoding*, with error handling performed according to *errors*. The error handling default is strict errors mode, where all encoding errors raise `ValueError`.

See also the `codecs` module in the Python Library Reference for files that support encodings. In 2.X, objects may provide a __unicode__() method that gives their Unicode string for unicode(*X*).

In Python 3.X, there is no separate type for Unicode—the str type represents all text (both 8-bit and richer Unicode), and the bytes type represents bytes of 8-bit binary data. Use normal str strings for Unicode text; bytes.decode() or str() to decode from raw bytes to Unicode according to an encoding; and normal open() file objects to process Unicode text files.

xrange([*start,*] *stop* [, *step*])

Like range(), but doesn't actually store the entire list all at once (rather, it generates one integer at a time). This is useful in for loops when there is a big range and little memory. It optimizes space, but generally has no speed benefit.

In Python 3.X, the original range() function is changed to return an iterable instead of producing a result list in memory, and thus subsumes and Python 2.X's xrange(), which is removed.

In addition, the file open() call has changed radically enough in Python 3.X that individual mention of Python 2.X's variant is warranted here (in Python 2.X, codecs.open() has many of the features in Python 3.X's open(), including support for Unicode encoding translations on transfers):

open(*filename* [, *mode,* [*bufsize*]])

Returns a new file object connected to the external file named *filename* (a string), or raises IOError if the open fails. The file name is mapped to the current working directory, unless it includes a directory path prefix. The first two arguments are generally the same as those for C's fopen() function, and the file is managed by the stdio system. With open(), file data is always represented as a normal str string in your script, containing bytes from the file. (codecs .open() interprets file content as encoded Unicode text, represented as unicode objects.)

mode defaults to 'r' if omitted, but can be 'r' for input; 'w' for output (truncating the file first); 'a' for append; and 'rb', 'wb', or 'ab' for binary files (to suppress line-end conversions to and from \n). On most systems, modes can also have a + appended to open in input/output updates mode (e.g., 'r+' to read/write, and 'w+' to read/write but initialize the file to empty).

bufsize defaults to an implementation-dependent value, but can be 0 for unbuffered, 1 for line-buffered, negative for system-default, or a given specific size. Buffered data transfers might not be immediately fulfilled (use file object flush() methods to force). See also the io module in Python's standard library: an alternative to file in 2.X, and the normal file interface for open() in 3.X.

Built-in Exceptions

This section describes exceptions predefined by Python that may be raised by Python or user code during a program's execution. It primarily presents the state of built-in exceptions in Python 3.3 —which introduces new classes for system-related errors that subsume prior generic classes with state information—but gives details common to most Python versions. See the Python 3.2 and 2.X subsections at the end of this section for version-specific differences.

Beginning with Python 1.5, all built-in exceptions are *class objects* (prior to 1.5 they were strings). Built-in exceptions are provided in the built-in scope namespace (see "Namespace and Scope Rules"), and many built-in exceptions have associated state information that provides exception details. User-defined exceptions are generally derived from this built-in set (see "The raise Statement").

Superclasses: Categories

The following exceptions are used only as superclasses for other exceptions:

`BaseException`
> The root superclass for all built-in exceptions. It is not meant to be directly inherited by user-defined classes; use `Exception` for this role instead. If `str()` is called on an instance of this class, the representation of the constructor argument(s) passed when creating the instance are returned (or the empty string if there were no such arguments). These instance constructor arguments are stored and made available in the instance's `args` attribute as a tuple. Subclasses inherit this protocol.

`Exception`
> The root superclass for all built-in and non-system-exiting exceptions. This is a direct subclass of `BaseException`.
>
> All user-defined exceptions should be derived (inherit) from this class. This derivation is required for user-defined exceptions in Python 3.X; Python 2.6 and 2.7 require this of new-style classes, but also allow standalone exception classes.
>
> `try` statements that catch this exception will catch all but system exit events, because this class is superclass to all exceptions but `SystemExit`, `KeyboardInterrupt`, and `GeneratorExit` (these three derive directly from `BaseException` instead).

`ArithmeticError`
> Arithmetic error exceptions category: the superclass of `OverflowError`, `ZeroDivisionError`, and `FloatingPointError`, and a subclass of `Exception`.

`BufferError`
> Raised when a buffer-related operation cannot be performed. A subclass of `Exception`.

LookupError

> Sequence and mapping index errors: the superclass for
> IndexError and KeyError, also raised for some Unicode en-
> coding lookup errors. A subclass of Exception.

OSError *(Python 3.3 version)*

> Raised when a system function triggers a system-related er-
> ror, including I/O and file operation failures. As of Python
> 3.3, this exception is a root class to a new set of descriptive
> system-related exceptions enumerated in "Specific OSError
> Exceptions", which subsume generic exceptions with state
> information used in 3.2 and earlier, described in "Python 3.2
> Built-in Exceptions".
>
> In Python 3.3, OSError is a subclass of Exception, and in-
> cludes common informational attributes that give system
> error details: errno (numeric code); strerror (string mes-
> sage); winerror (on Windows); and filename (for exceptions
> involving file paths). In 3.3, this class incorporates the for-
> mer EnvironmentError, IOError, WindowsError, VMSError,
> socket.error, select.error, and mmap.error, and is a syn-
> onym to os.error. See the latter in "The os System Mod-
> ule" for additional attribute details.

Specific Exceptions

The following classes are more specific exceptions that are
actually raised. In addition, NameError, RuntimeError, Syntax
Error, ValueError, and Warning are both specific exceptions and
category superclasses to other built-in exceptions:

AssertionError

> Raised when an assert statement's test is false.

AttributeError

> Raised on attribute reference or assignment failure.

EOFError

Raised when the immediate end-of-file is hit by input() (or raw_input() in Python 2.X). File object read methods return an empty object at end of file instead of raising this.

FloatingPointError

Raised on floating-point operation failure.

GeneratorExit

Raised when a generator's close() method is called. This directly inherits from BaseException instead of Exception since it is not an error.

ImportError

Raised when an import or from fails to find a module or attribute. As of Python 3.3, instances include name and path attributes identifying the module that triggered the error, passed as keyword arguments to the constructor.

IndentationError

Raised when improper indentation is found in source code. Derived from SyntaxError.

IndexError

Raised on out-of-bounds sequence offsets (fetch or assign). Slice indexes are silently adjusted to fall in the allowed range; if an index is not an integer, TypeError is raised.

KeyError

Raised on references to nonexistent mapping keys (fetch). Assignment to a nonexistent key creates that key.

KeyboardInterrupt

Raised on user entry of the interrupt key (normally Ctrl-C or Delete). During execution, a check for interrupts is made regularly. This exception inherits directly from Base Exception to prevent it from being accidentally caught by code that catches Exception and thus prevents interpreter exit.

MemoryError

> Raised on recoverable memory exhaustion. This causes a stack trace to be displayed if a runaway program was its cause.

NameError

> Raised on failures to find a local or global unqualified name.

NotImplementedError

> Raised on failures to define expected protocols. Abstract class methods may raise this when they require a method to be redefined. Derived from RuntimeError. (This is not to be confused with NotImplemented, a special built-in object returned by some operator-overloading methods when operand types are not supported; see "Operator Overloading Methods".)

OverflowError

> Raised on excessively large arithmetic operation results. This cannot occur for integers as they support arbitrary precision. Due to constraints in the underlying C language, most floating-point operations are also not checked for overflow.

ReferenceError

> Raised in conjunction with *weak references*; tools for maintaining references to objects which do not prevent their reclamation (e.g., caches). See the weakref module in the Python standard library.

RuntimeError

> A rarely used catch-all exception.

StopIteration

> Raised at the end of values progression in iterator objects. Raised by the next(I) built-in and I.__next__() methods (named I.next() in Python 2.X).
>
> As of Python 3.3, instances include a value attribute, which either reflects an explicit constructor positional argument, or is automatically set to the return value given in a generator

function's return statement that ends its iteration. This value defaults to None, is also available in the exception's normal args tuple, and is unused by automatic iterations. Because generator functions must return *no* value prior to 3.3 (and generate syntax errors if they try), use of this extension is not compatible with earlier 2.X and 3.X versions. See also "The yield Statement".

SyntaxError

Raised when parsers encounter a syntax error. This may occur during import operations, calls to eval() and exec(), and when reading code in a top-level script file or standard input. Instances of this class have attributes filename, lineno, offset, and text for access to details; str() of the exception instance returns only the basic message.

SystemError

Raised on interpreter internal errors that are not serious enough to shut down (these should be reported).

SystemExit

Raised on a call to sys.exit(N). If not handled, the Python interpreter exits, and no stack traceback is printed. If the passed value *N* is an integer, it specifies the program's system exit status (passed on to C's exit function); if it is None or omitted, the exit status is 0 (success); if it has another type, the object's value is printed and the exit status is 1 (failure). Derived directly from BaseException to prevent it from being accidentally caught by code that catches Exception and thus prevents interpreter exit. See also sys.exit() in "The sys Module".

sys.exit() raises this exception so that clean-up handlers (finally clauses of try statements) are executed, and so that a debugger can execute a script without losing control. The os._exit() function exits immediately when needed (e.g., in the child process after a call to fork()). Also see the atexit module in the standard library for exit function specification.

TabError

> Raised when an improper mixture of spaces and tabs is found in source code. Derived from `IndentationError`.

TypeError

> Raised when an operation or function is applied to an object of inappropriate type.

UnboundLocalError

> Raised on references to local names that have not yet been assigned a value. Derived from `NameError`.

UnicodeError

> Raised on Unicode-related encoding or decoding errors; a superclass category, and a subclass of `ValueError`. Hint: some Unicode tools may also raise `LookupError`.

UnicodeEncodeError

UnicodeDecodeError

UnicodeTranslateError

> Raised on Unicode-related processing errors; subclasses of `UnicodeError`.

ValueError

> Raised when a built-in operation or function receives an argument that has the correct type but an inappropriate value, and the situation is not described by a more specific exception like `IndexError`.

ZeroDivisionError

> Raised on division or modulus operations with value 0 as the right-side operand.

Specific OSError Exceptions

Available in Python 3.3 and later, the following subclasses of `OSError` identify system errors, and correspond to system error codes available in `EnvironmentError` in earlier Pythons (see "Python 3.2 Built-in Exceptions"). See also `OSError` in

"Superclasses: Categories" for informational attributes common to its subclasses here:

BlockingIOError
> Raised when an operation would block on an object set for nonblocking operation. Has additional attribute characters_written, the number of characters written to the stream before it blocked.

ChildProcessError
> Raised when an operation on a child process failed.

ConnectionError
> Superclass for connection-related exceptions BrokenPipe Error, ConnectionAbortedError, ConnectionRefusedError, and ConnectionResetError.

BrokenPipeError
> Raised when trying to write on a pipe while the other end has been closed, or trying to write on a socket that has been shut down for writing.

ConnectionAbortedError
> Raised when a connection attempt is aborted by the peer.

ConnectionRefusedError
> Raised when a connection attempt is refused by the peer.

ConnectionResetError
> Raised when a connection is reset by the peer.

FileExistsError
> Raised when trying to create a file or directory which already exists.

FileNotFoundError
> Raised when a file or directory is requested but doesn't exist.

InterruptedError
> Raised when a system call is interrupted by an incoming signal.

`IsADirectoryError`
> Raised when a file operation such as `os.remove()` is requested on a directory.

`NotADirectoryError`
> Raised when a directory operation such as `os.listdir()` is requested on a nondirectory.

`PermissionError`
> Raised for operations run without adequate access rights (e.g., file system permissions).

`ProcessLookupError`
> Raised when a process doesn't exist.

`TimeoutError`
> Raised when a system function times out at the system level.

Warning Category Exceptions

The following exceptions are used as warning categories:

`Warning`
> The superclass for all of the following warnings; a direct subclass of `Exception`.

`UserWarning`
> Warnings generated by user code.

`DeprecationWarning`
> Warnings about deprecated features.

`PendingDeprecationWarning`
> Warnings about features that will be deprecated in the future.

`SyntaxWarning`
> Warnings about dubious syntax.

`RuntimeWarning`
> Warnings about dubious runtime behavior.

FutureWarning
> Warnings about constructs that will change semantically in the future.

ImportWarning
> Warnings about probable mistakes in module imports.

UnicodeWarning
> Warnings related to Unicode.

BytesWarning
> Warnings related to bytes and buffer (memory-view) objects.

ResourceWarning
> Added as of Python 3.2, the superclass for warnings related to resource usage.

Warnings Framework

Warnings are issued when future language changes might break existing code in a future Python release, and in other contexts. Warnings may be configured to print messages, raise exceptions, or be ignored. The warnings framework can be used to issue warnings by calling the warnings.warn() function:

```
warnings.warn("usage obsolete", DeprecationWarning)
```

In addition, you can add filters to disable certain warnings. You can apply a regular expression pattern to a message or module name to suppress warnings with varying degrees of generality. For example, you can suppress a warning about the use of the deprecated regex module by calling:

```
import warnings
warnings.filterwarnings(action = 'ignore',
                        message='.*regex module*',
                        category=DeprecationWarning,
                        module = '__main__')
```

This adds a filter that affects only warnings of the class DeprecationWarning triggered in the __main__ module, applies a regular expression to match only the message that names the regex module being deprecated, and causes such warnings to be ignored. Warnings can also be printed only once, printed every time the offending code is executed, or turned into exceptions that will cause the program to stop (unless the exceptions are caught). See the warnings module documentation in Python's manual (version 2.1 and later) for more information. See also the -W argument in "Python Command Options".

Python 3.2 Built-in Exceptions

In Python 3.2 and earlier, the following additional exceptions are available. As of Python 3.3, they have been merged into OSError. They are retained in 3.3 for compatibility, but may be removed in future releases:

EnvironmentError

> The category for exceptions that occur outside Python: the superclass for IOError and OSError, and a subclass of Exception. The raised instance includes informational attributes errno and strerror (and possible filename for exceptions involving file paths), which are also in args, and give system error code and message details.

IOError

> Raised on I/O or file-related operation failures. Derived from EnvironmentError with state information described earlier in this list.

OSError *(Python 3.2 version)*

> Raised on os module errors (its os.error exception). Derived from EnvironmentError with state information described earlier in this list.

VMSError

> Raised on VMS-specific errors; a subclass of OSError.

WindowsError

> Raised on Windows-specific errors; a subclass of OSError.

Python 2.X Built-in Exceptions

The set of available exceptions, as well as the shape of the exception class hierarchy, varies slightly in Python 2.X from the 3.X description of the preceding sections. For example, in Python 2.X:

- `Exception` is the topmost root class (not `BaseException`, which is absent in Python 2.X).

- `StandardError` is an additional `Exception` subclass, and is a root class above all built-in exceptions except `SystemExit`.

See Python 2.X library manuals for full details for your version.

Built-in Attributes

Some objects export special attributes that are predefined by Python. The following is a partial list because many types have unique attributes all their own; see the entries for specific types in the Python Library Reference:[6]

`X.__dict__`
> Dictionary used to store object *X*'s writable (changeable) attributes.

`I.__class__`
> Class object from which instance *I* was generated. In version 2.2 and later, this also applies to types, and most objects have a `__class__` attribute (e.g., `[].__class__ == list == type([])`).

---

6. As of Python 2.1, you can also attach arbitrary user-defined attributes to *function* objects, simply by assigning them values; see "Function defaults and attributes". Python 2.X also supports special attributes `I.__meth ods__` and `I.__members__`: lists of method and data member names for instances of some built-in types. These are removed in Python 3.X; use the built-in `dir()` function.

`C.__bases__`
> Tuple of class *C*'s base classes, as listed in *C*'s class statement header.

`C.__mro__`
> The computed MRO path through new-style class *C*'s tree (see "New-style classes: MRO").

`X.__name__`
> Object *X*'s name as a string; for classes, the name in the statement header; for modules, the name as used in imports, or "`__main__`" for the module at the top level of a program (e.g., the main file run to launch a program).

Standard Library Modules

Standard library modules are always available but must be imported to be used in client modules. To access them, use one of these formats:

- `import` *module*, and fetch attribute names (*module.name*)

- `from` *module* `import` *name*, and use module names unqualified (*name*)

- `from` *module* `import *`, and use module names unqualified (*name*)

For instance, to use name `argv` in the `sys` module, either use `import sys` and name `sys.argv` or use `from sys import argv` and name `argv`. The former full form—*module.name*—is used in content list headers here only to provide context in multipage listings; descriptions often use just *name*.

There are hundreds of standard library modules, all of which are at least as prone to change as the language itself. Accordingly, the following sections *are not exhaustive*, and generally document only commonly used names in commonly used modules. See Python's Library Reference for a more complete reference to standard library modules.

In all of the following module sections:

- Listed export names followed by parentheses are *functions* that must be called; others are simple attributes (i.e., variable names in modules that are fetched, not called).

- Module contents document the modules' state in *Python 3.X*, but generally apply to both 3.X and 2.X except as noted; see Python manuals for further information on version-specific differences.

The sys Module

The sys module contains *interpreter-related tools*: items related to the interpreter or its process in both Python 3.X and 2.X. It also provides access to some environment components, such as the command line, standard streams, and so on. See also os in "The os System Module" for additional process-related tools:

sys.argv
> Command-line argument strings list: [*scriptname, arguments...*]. Similar to C's argv array. argv[0] is either the script file's name (possibly with a full path); the string '-c' for the -c command-line option; a module's path name for the -m option; '-' for the – option; or the empty string if no script name or command option was passed. See also "Command-Line Program Specification".

sys.byteorder
> Indicates the native byte order (e.g., 'big' for big-endian, 'little' for little-endian).

sys.builtin_module_names
> Tuple of string names of C modules compiled into this Python interpreter.

sys.copyright
> String containing the Python interpreter copyright.

`sys.displayhook(value)`

> Called by Python to display result values in interactive sessions; assign `sys.displayhook` to a one-argument function to customize output.

`sys.dont_write_bytecode`

> While this is true, Python won't try to write *.pyc* or *.pyo* files on the import of source modules (see also `-B` command-line option in "Python Command-Line Usage" to select at launch).

`sys.excepthook(type, value, traceback)`

> Called by Python to display uncaught exception details to *stderr*; assign `sys.excepthook` to a three-argument function to customize exception displays.

`sys.exc_info()`

> Returns tuple of three values describing the exception currently being handled: (`type, value, traceback`), where `type` is the exception class, `value` is the instance of the exception class raised, and `traceback` is an object that gives access to the runtime call stack as it existed when the exception occurred. Specific to current thread. Subsumes `exc_type`, `exc_value`, and `exc_traceback` in Python 1.5 and later (all three of which are present in earlier Python 2.X, but removed completely in Python 3.X). See the `traceback` module in the Python Library Reference for processing traceback objects, and "The try Statement" for more on exceptions.

`sys.exec_prefix`

> Assign to a string giving the site-specific directory prefix where the platform-dependent Python files are installed; defaults to */usr/local* or a build-time argument. Used to locate shared library modules (in *<exec_prefix>/lib/ python<version>/lib-dynload*) and configuration files.

`sys.executable`

> String giving the full file pathname of the Python interpreter program running the caller.

`sys.exit([N])`

Exits from a Python process with status *N* (default 0) by raising a `SystemExit` built-in exception (which can be caught in a `try` statement and ignored if needed). See also `SystemExit` in ("Built-in Exceptions") for more usage details, and the `os._exit()` function (in "The os System Module") for a related tool that exits immediately without exception processing (useful in child processes after an `os.fork()`). Also see the `atexit` module in the Python standard library for general exit function specification.

`sys.flags`

Values of Python command-line options, one attribute per option (see Python manuals).

`sys.float_info`

Details of Python floating-point implementation via attributes (see Python manuals).

`sys.getcheckinterval()`

In Python 3.1 and earlier, returns the interpreter's "check interval" (see `setcheckinterval()` later in this list). Superseded in Python 3.2 and later by `getswitchinterval()`.

`sys.getdefaultencoding()`

Returns the name of the current default string encoding used by the Unicode implementation.

`sys.getfilesystemencoding()`

Returns the name of the encoding used to convert Unicode filenames into system file names, or `None` if the system default encoding is used.

`sys._getframe([depth])`

Returns a frame object from the Python call stack (see the Python Library Reference).

`sys.getrefcount(object)`

Returns *object*'s current reference count value (+1 for the call's argument itself).

`sys.getrecursionlimit()`

> Returns the maximum depth limit of the Python call stack; see also `setrecursionlimit()`, later in this list.

`sys.getsizeof(object [, default])`

> Returns the size of an *object* in bytes. The object can be any type of object. All built-in objects return correct results, but third-party extension results are implementation specific. *default* provides a value that will be returned if the object type does not implement the size retrieval interface.

`sys.getswitchinterval()`

> In Python 3.2 and later, returns the interpreter's current thread switch interval setting (see `setswitchinterval()` later in this list). In Python 3.1 and earlier, use `getcheck interval()`.

`sys.getwindowsversion()`

> Return an object describing the Windows version currently running (see Python manuals).

`sys.hexversion`

> Python version number, encoded as a single integer (perhaps best viewed with the `hex()` built-in function). Increases with each new release.

`sys.implementation`

> Available as of Python 3.3, an object giving information about the implementation of the currently running Python interpreter (name, version, etc.). See Python manuals.

`sys.int_info`

> Details of Python integer implementation via attributes (see Python manuals).

`sys.intern(string)`

> Enters *string* in the table of "interned" strings and returns the interned string—the string itself or a copy. Interning strings provides a small performance improvement for dictionary lookup: if both the keys in a dictionary and the lookup key are interned, key comparisons (after hashing)

can be done by comparing pointers instead of strings. Normally, names used in Python programs are automatically interned, and the dictionaries used to hold module, class, and instance attributes have interned keys.

`sys.last_type`, `sys.last_value`, `sys.last_traceback`
Type, value, and traceback objects of last uncaught exception (mostly for postmortem debugging).

`sys.maxsize`
An integer giving the maximum value a variable of type `Py_ssize_t` can take. It's usually $2**31 - 1$ on a 32-bit platform and $2**63 - 1$ on a 64-bit platform.

`sys.maxunicode`
An integer giving the largest supported code point for a Unicode character. In Python 3.3 and later, this is always `1114111` (`0x10FFFF` in hexadecimal) due to 3.3's flexible and variable-size string storage system. Prior to 3.3, the value of this depends on the configuration option that specifies whether Unicode characters are stored as UCS-2 or UCS-4, and may be `0xFFFF` or `0x10FFFF`.

`sys.modules`
Dictionary of modules that are already loaded; there is one *name*: *object* entry per module. Hint: this dictionary may be changed to impact future imports (e.g., `del sys.modules ['name']` forces a module to be reloaded on next import).

`sys.path`
List of strings specifying module import search path. Initialized from `PYTHONPATH` shell variable, any *.pth* path files, and any installation-dependent defaults. Hint: this attribute and its list may both be changed to impact future imports (e.g., `sys.path.append('C:\\dir')` adds a directory to the module search path dynamically).

The first item, `path[0]`, is the directory containing the script that was used to invoke the Python interpreter. If the script directory is not available (e.g., if the interpreter is invoked interactively or if the script is read from standard input), path[0] is the empty string, which directs Python to search modules in the current working directory first. The script directory is inserted before the entries inserted from PYTHONPATH. See also "The import Statement".

sys.platform

String identifying the system on which Python is running: 'win32', 'darwin', 'linux2', 'cygwin', 'os2', 'freebsd8', 'sunos5', 'PalmOS3', etc. Useful for tests in platform-dependent code.

This is 'win32' for all current flavors of Windows, but test sys.platform[:3]=='win' or sys.platform.startswith ('win') for generality. As of Python 3.3, all Linux platforms are 'linux', but scripts should similarly test for this with *str*.startswith('linux') as it was formerly either 'linux2' or 'linux3'.

sys.prefix

Assign to a string giving the site-specific directory prefix, where platform-independent Python files are installed; defaults to */usr/local* or a build-time argument. Python library modules are installed in the directory *<prefix>/lib/ python<version>*; platform-independent header files are stored in *<prefix>/include/python<version>*.

sys.ps1

String specifying primary prompt in interactive mode; defaults to >>> unless assigned.

sys.ps2

String specifying secondary prompt for compound statement continuations, in interactive mode; defaults to ... unless assigned.

sys.setcheckinterval(*reps*)

Superseded in Python 3.2 and later by setswitchinterval() (covered in this list). In 3.2 and later, this function is still present but has no effect, as the implementation of thread switching and asynchronous tasks was rewritten.

In Python 3.1 and earlier, called to set how often the interpreter checks for periodic tasks (e.g., thread switches, signal handlers) to *reps*, measured in virtual machine instructions (default is 100). In general, a Python statement translates to multiple virtual machine instructions. Lower values maximize thread responsiveness but also maximize thread switch overhead.

sys.setdefaultencoding(*name*)

Removed as of Python 3.2. Call to set the current default string encoding used by the Unicode implementation to *name*. Intended for use by the site module and is available during start-up only.

sys.setprofile(*func*)

Call to set the system profile function to *func*: the profiler's "hook" (not run for each line). See the Python Library Reference for details.

sys.setrecursionlimit(*depth*)

Call to set maximum depth of the Python call stack to *depth*. This limit prevents infinite recursion from causing an overflow of the C stack and crashing Python. The default is 1,000 on Windows, but this may vary. Higher values may be required for deeply recursive functions.

sys.setswitchinterval(*interval*)

In Python 3.2 and later, sets the interpreter's thread switch interval to *interval*, given in seconds This is a floating-point value (e.g., 0.005 is 5 milliseconds) that determines the ideal duration of the time slices allocated to concurrently running Python threads. The actual value can be higher, especially if long-running internal functions or methods are used, and the choice of thread scheduled at the end of the interval is made by the operating system. (The Python interpreter does not have its own scheduler.)

In Python 3.1 and earlier, use `setcheckinterval()` instead (covered in this list).

`sys.settrace(func)`

Call to set the system trace function to *func*. This is the program location or state change callback "hook" used by debuggers, etc. See the Python Library Reference for details.

`sys.stdin`

A preopened file object, initially connected to the standard input stream, *stdin*. Can be assigned to any object with read methods to reset input within a script (e.g., `sys.stdin = MyObj()`). Used for interpreter input, including the `input()` built-in function (and `raw_input()` in Python 2.X).

`sys.stdout`

A preopened file object, initially connected to the standard output stream, *stdout*. Can be assigned to any object with write methods to reset output within a script (e.g., `sys.stdout=open('log', 'a')`). Used for some prompts and the `print()` built-in function (and print statement in Python 2.X). Use `PYTHONIOENCODING` to override the platform-dependent encoding if needed (see "Python Environment Variables"), and `-u` for unbuffered streams (see "Python Command Options").

`sys.stderr`

A preopened file object, initially connected to the standard error stream, *stderr*. Can be assigned to any object with write methods to reset stderr within a script (e.g., `sys.stderr=wrappedsocket`). Used for interpreter prompts/errors.

`sys.__stdin__`, `sys.__stdout__`, `sys.__stderr__`

Original values of stdin, stderr, and stdout at program start (e.g., for restores as a last resort; normally, when assigning to `sys.stdout`, etc., save the old value and restore it in a finally clause). Note: these can be None for GUI apps on Windows with no console.

`sys.thread_info`

> Details of Python's thread implementation via attributes; new in Python 3.3 (see Python manuals).

`sys.tracebacklimit`

> Maximum number of traceback levels to print on uncaught exceptions; defaults to `1,000` unless assigned.

`sys.sys.version`

> String containing the version number of the Python interpreter.

`sys.version_info`

> Tuple containing five version identification components: major, minor, micro, release level, and serial. For Python 3.0.1, this is (`3, 0, 1, 'final', 0`). In recent releases only, this is a named tuple, whose components may be accessed as either tuple items or attribute names; for Python 3.3.0, this displays `sys.version_info(major=3, minor=3, micro=0, releaselevel='final', serial=0)`. See the Python Library Reference for more details.

`sys.winver`

> Version number used to form registry keys on Windows platforms (available only on Windows; see the Python Library Reference).

The string Module

The `string` module defines constants and variables for processing *string objects*. See also "Strings" for more on the string template substitution and formatting tools `Template` and `Formatter` defined in this module.

Functions and Classes

As of Python 2.0, most functions in this module are also available as *methods* of string objects; method-based calls are more efficient, are preferred in 2.X, and are the only option retained in 3.X. See "Strings" for more details and a list of all available string methods not repeated here. Only items unique to the string module are listed in this section:

`string.capwords(s, sep=None)`
> Split the argument *s* into words using *s*.split(), capitalize each word using *s*.capitalize(), and join the capitalized words using *s*.join(). If the optional argument sep is absent or None, runs of whitespace characters are replaced by a single space, and leading and trailing whitespace is removed; otherwise sep is used to split and join the words.

`string.maketrans(from, to)`
> Returns a translation table suitable for passing to bytes.translate() that will map each character in *from* into the character at the same position in *to*; *from* and *to* must have the same length.

`string.Formatter`
> Class that allows creation of custom formatters using the same mechanism as the str.format() method, described in "String formatting method".

`string.Template`
> String template substitution class, described in "Template string substitution".

Constants

`string.ascii_letters`
> The string ascii_lowercase + ascii_uppercase.

`string.ascii_lowercase`
> The string 'abcdefghijklmnopqrstuvwxyz'; not locale-dependent and will not change.

`string.ascii_uppercase`
> The string 'ABCDEFGHIJKLMNOPQRSTUVWXYZ'; not locale-dependent and will not change.

`string.digits`
> The string '0123456789'.

`string.hexdigits`
> The string `'0123456789abcdefABCDEF'`.

`string.octdigits`
> The string `'01234567'`.

`string.printable`
> Combination of `digits`, `ascii_letters`, `punctuation`, and `whitespace`.

`string.punctuation`
> String of characters that are considered punctuation characters in the locale.

`string.whitespace`
> String containing space, tab, line feed, return, vertical tab, and form feed: `' \t\n\r\v\f'`.

The os System Module

The `os` module is the primary *operating system* (OS) services interface in both Python 3.X and 2.X. It provides generic OS support and a standard, platform-independent set of OS utilities. The `os` module includes tools for environments, processes, files, shell commands, and much more. It also includes a nested submodule, `os.path`, which provides a portable interface to directory processing tools.

Scripts that use `os` and `os.path` for systems programming are generally *portable* across most Python platforms. However, some `os` exports are not available on all platforms (e.g., `os.fork()` is available on Unix and Cygwin, but not in the standard Windows version of Python). Because the portability of such calls can change over time, consult the Python Library Reference for platform details.

The following sections highlight commonly used tools in this module. *This is a partial list*: see Python's standard library manual for full details on the over 200 tools in this module on some platforms, as well as platform and version differences omitted here. Subsections here reflect this large module's functional areas:

- *Administrative Tools*: module-related exports
- *Portability Constants*: directory and search-path constants
- *Shell Commands*: running command lines and files
- *Environment Tools*: execution environment and context
- *File Descriptor Tools*: processing files by their descriptors
- *File Pathname Tools*: processing files by their path names
- *Process Control*: creating and managing processes
- *The os.path Module*: directory path name-related services

See also these *related system modules* in Python's standard library, covered in Python manuals except as noted: sys—interpreter process tools (see "The sys Module"); subprocess—spawned command control (see "The subprocess Module"); threading and queue—multithreading tools (see "Threading Modules"); socket—networking and IPC (see "Internet Modules and Tools"); glob—filename expansion (e.g., glob.glob('*.py')); tempfile—temporary files; signal—signal handling; multi processing—threading-like API for processes; and getopt, optparse, and, in 3.2 and later, argparse—command-line processing.

Administrative Tools

Following are some miscellaneous module-related exports:

os.error

An alias for the built-in OSError exception: see "Built-in Exceptions". Raised for all os module-related errors. This exception has two attributes: errno, the numeric error code per POSIX (e.g., the value of the C errno variable); and strerror, the corresponding error message provided by the operating system, and as formatted by underlying C functions (e.g., by perror(), and as for os.strerror()). For exceptions that involve a file pathname (e.g., chdir(), unlink()), the exception instance also contains the attribute filename, the filename passed in. See the module errno in the Python Library Reference for names of the error codes defined by the underlying OS.

os.name

Name of OS-specific modules whose names are copied to the top level of os (e.g., posix, nt, mac, os2, ce, or java). See also sys.platform in section "The sys Module".

os.path

Nested module for portable pathname-related utilities. For example, os.path.split() is a platform-independent directory name tool that performs appropriate platform-specific action.

Portability Constants

This section describes *file portability tools*, for directory and search paths, line feeds, and more. They are automatically set to the appropriate value for the platform on which a script is running, and are useful for both parsing and constructing platform-dependent strings. See also "The os.path Module":

os.curdir

String used to represent current directory (e.g., . for Windows and POSIX, : for Macintosh).

os.pardir

String used to represent parent directory (e.g., .. for POSIX, :: for Macintosh).

os.sep

String used to separate directories (e.g., / for Unix, \ for Windows, or : for Macintosh).

os.altsep

Alternative separator string or None (e.g., / for Windows).

os.extsep

> The character that separates the base filename from the extension (e.g., .).

os.pathsep

> Character used to separate search path components, as in the PATH and PYTHONPATH shell variable settings (e.g., ; for Windows, : for Unix).

os.defpath

> Default search path used by os.exec*p* calls if there is no PATH setting in the shell.

os.linesep

> String used to terminate lines on current platform (e.g., \n for POSIX, \r for Mac OS, and \r\n for Windows). Not required writing lines in text mode files—use the file object's auto-translation of '\n' (see open() in "Built-in Functions").

os.devnull

> The file path of the "null" device (for text be discarded). This is '/dev/null' for POSIX, and 'nul' for Windows (also in the os.path submodule).

Shell Commands

These functions run *command lines or files* in the underlying operating system. In Python 2.X, this module has os.popen2/3/4 calls, which have been replaced in Python 3.X by subprocess.Popen—a tool that generally offers finer-grained control over spawned commands (see "The subprocess Module"). Hint: do not use these tools to launch untrustworthy shell command strings, as they may run any command allowed for the Python process:

os.system(cmd)

> Executes a shell command-line string cmd in a subshell process. Returns the exit status of the spawned process. Unlike popen(), does not connect to cmd's standard streams via

pipes. Hint: add a & at the end of *cmd* to run the command in the background on Unix (e.g., os.system('python main.py &')); use a Windows (DOS) start command to launch programs easily on Windows (e.g., os.system ('start file.html')).

os.startfile(*filepathname*)

Starts a file with its associated application. Acts like double-clicking the file in Windows Explorer or giving the filename as an argument to a Windows start command (e.g., with os.system('start *path*')). The file is opened in the application with which its extension is associated; the call does not wait, and does not generally pop up a Windows console window (a.k.a. *Command Prompt*). Windows only, added in version 2.0.

os.popen(*cmd*, mode='r', buffering=None)

Opens a pipe to or from the shell command-line string *cmd*, to send or capture data. Returns an open file object, which can be used to either read from *cmd*'s standard output stream *stdout* (mode 'r', the default) or write to *cmd*'s standard input stream *stdin* (mode 'w'). For example, dirlist = os.popen ('ls -l *.py').read() reads the output of a Unix ls command.

cmd is any command string you can type at your system's console or shell prompt. mode can be 'r' or 'w' and defaults to 'r'. buffering is the same as in the built-in open() function. *cmd* runs independently; its exit status is returned by the resulting file object's close() method, except that None is returned if exit status is 0 (no errors). Use readline() or file object iteration to read output line by line (and possibly interleave operations more fully).

Python 2.X also has variants popen2(), popen3(), and popen4() to connect to other streams of the spawned command (e.g., popen2() returns a tuple (*child_stdin*, *child_stdout*)). In Python 3.X, these calls are removed; use subprocess.Popen() instead. The subprocess module in version 2.4 and later allows scripts to spawn new processes, connect to their streams, and obtain their return codes (see "The subprocess Module").

os.spawn*(*args...*)

A family of functions for spawning programs and commands. See "Process Control" ahead, as well as the Python Library Reference for more details. The subprocess module is an alternative to these calls (see "The subprocess Module").

Environment Tools

These attributes export *execution context*: shell environment, current directory, and so on:

os.environ

The shell environment variable dictionary-like object. os.environ['USER'] is the value of variable USER in the shell (equivalent to $USER in Unix and %USER% in Windows). Initialized on program start-up. Changes made to os.environ by key assignment are exported outside Python using a call to C's putenv() and are inherited by any processes that are later spawned in any way, as well as any linked-in C code. See also Python manuals for the os.environb environment bytes interface in Python 3.2 and later.

os.putenv(*varname, value*)

Sets the shell environment variable named *varname* to the string *value*. Affects subprocesses started with system(), popen(), spawnv(), fork() and execv(), and more. Assignment to os.environ keys automatically calls os.putenv(), but os.putenv() calls don't update os.environ, so os.environ is preferred.

os.getenv(*varname*, default=None)

Return the value of the environment variable *varname* if it exists, else *default*. At present, this simply indexes the preloaded environment dictionary, with os.environ.get (*varname, default*). *varname, default*, and the result are str;

see also Python's manuals for Unicode encoding rules, and `os.getenvb()` for a bytes equivalent as of Python 3.2.

`os.getcwd()`

Returns the current working directory name as a string.

`os.chdir(path)`

Changes the current working directory for this process to *path*, a directory name string. Future file operations are relative to the new current working directory. Hint: this does not update `sys.path` used for module imports, although its first entry may be a generic current working directory designator.

`os.strerror(code)`

Returns an error message corresponding to *code*.

`os.times()`

Returns a five-tuple containing elapsed CPU time information for the calling process in floating-point seconds: (*user-time*, *system-time*, *child-user-time*, *child-system-time*, *elapsed-real-time*). Also see "The time Module".

`os.umask(mask)`

Sets the numeric umask to *mask* and returns the prior value.

`os.uname()`

Returns OS name tuple of strings: (*systemname*, *nodename*, *release*, *version*, *machine*).

File Descriptor Tools

The following functions process *files by their file descriptors*, where *fd* is a file descriptor integer. os module file descriptor-based files are meant for low-level file tasks and are not the same as `stdio` file *objects* returned by the built-in `open()` function. File *objects*, not the file *descriptors* here, should normally be used for most file processing. See `open()` in "Built-in Functions" for details. If needed, `os.fdopen()` and the file object's `fileno()` method convert between the two forms, and the built-in `open()` function accepts a file descriptor in 3.X.

`os.close(fd)`

> Closes file descriptor *fd* (not a file object).

`os.dup(fd)`

> Returns duplicate of file descriptor *fd*.

`os.dup2(fd, fd2)`

> Copies file descriptor *fd* to *fd2* (close *fd2* first if open).

`os.fdopen(fd, *args, **kwargs)`

> Returns a built-in `stdio` file *object* connected to file descriptor *fd* (an integer). This is an alias for the `open()` built-in function and accepts the same arguments, except that first argument of `fdopen()` must always be an integer file descriptor (see `open()` in "Built-in Functions"). A conversion from file descriptor-based files to file objects is normally created automatically by the built-in `open()` function. Hint: use *fileobject*.`fileno()` to convert a file object to a file descriptor.

`os.fstat(fd)`

> Returns status for file descriptor *fd* (like `os.stat()`).

`os.ftruncate(fd, length)`

> Truncates the file corresponding to file descriptor *fd* so that it is at most *length* bytes in size.

`os.isatty(fd)`

> Returns `True` if file descriptor *fd* is open and connected to a tty-like (interactive) device, else `False` (may return `1` or `0` in older Pythons).

`os.lseek(fd, pos, how)`
> Sets the current position of file descriptor *fd* to *pos* (for random access). how can be 0 to set the position relative to the start of the file, 1 to set it relative to the current position, or 2 to set it relative to the end.

`os.open(filename, flags[, mode=0o777], [dir_fd=None])`
> Opens a file descriptor-based file and returns the file descriptor—an integer that may be passed to other os module file operation calls, not a stdio file object. Intended for low-level file tasks only; not the same as the built-in open() function, which is preferred for most file processing (see "Built-in Functions").
>
> *filename* is the file's possibly-relative path name string. *flags* is a bitmask: use | to combine both platform-neutral and platform-specific flag constants defined in the os module (see Table 18). mode defaults to 0o777 (octal), and the current umask value is first masked out. dir_fd is new in Python 3.3, and supports paths relative to directory file descriptors (see Python manuals). Hint: os.open() may be used with the os.O_EXCL flag to portably lock files for concurrent updates or other process synchronization.

`os.pipe()`
> Create an anonymous pipe. See "Process Control".

`os.read(fd, n)`
> Reads at most *n* bytes from file descriptor *fd* and returns those bytes as a string.

`os.write(fd, str)`
> Writes all bytes in string *str* to file descriptor *fd*.

Table 18. Sample or-able flags for os.open (all os.flag)

O_APPEND	O_EXCL	O_RDONLY	O_TRUNC
O_BINARY	O_NDELAY	O_RDWR	O_WRONLY
O_CREAT	O_NOCTTY	O_RSYNC	
O_DSYNC	O_NONBLOCK	O_SYNC	

File Pathname Tools

The following functions *process files* by their pathnames, in which *path* is a string pathname of a file. See also "The os.path Module". In Python 2.X, this module also includes temporary file tools that have been replaced with the tempfile module in Python 3.X. As of Python 3.3, some of these tools have grown an additional and optional dir_fd argument not shown here, to support paths relative to directory file descriptors; see Python manuals for details:

os.chdir(*path*)

os.getcwd()

> Current working directory tools. See "Environment Tools".

os.chmod(*path, mode*)

> Changes mode of file *path* to numeric *mode*.

os.chown(*path, uid, gid*)

> Changes owner/group IDs of *path* to numeric *uid/gid*.

os.link(*srcpath, dstpath*)

> Creates a hard link to file *srcpath*, named *dstpath*.

os.listdir(*path*)

> Returns a list of names of all the entries in the directory *path*. A fast and portable alternative to the glob.glob (*pattern*) call and to running shell listing commands with os.popen(). See also module glob in Python manuals for filename pattern expansion, and os.walk() later in this section for full directory tree walking.

> In Python 3.X, this call is passed and returns bytes instead of str to suppress Unicode filename decoding per platform default (this behavior also applies to glob.glob() and os.walk()). In Python 3.2 and later, *path* defaults to "." if omitted, the current working directory.

os.lstat(*path*)

> Like os.stat(), but does not follow symbolic links.

`os.mkfifo(path [, mode=0o666])`

> Creates a *FIFO* (a named pipe) identified by string *path* with access permission given by numeric *mode* (but does not open it). The default mode is 0o666 (octal). The current umask value is first masked out from the mode. This call has a dir_fd optional keyword-only argument in 3.3.
>
> FIFOs are pipes that live in the filesystem and can be opened and processed like regular files, but support synchronized access between independently started clients and servers, by common filename. FIFOs exist until deleted. This call is currently available on Unix-like platforms, including Cygwin on Windows, but not in standard Windows Python. Sockets can often achieve similar goals (see the socket module in "Internet Modules and Tools" and Python manuals).

`os.mkdir(path [, mode])`

> Makes a directory called *path*, with the given *mode*. The default mode is 0o777 (octal).

`os.makedirs(path [, mode])`

> Recursive directory-creation function. Like mkdir(), but makes all intermediate-level directories needed to contain the leaf directory. Throws an exception if the leaf directory already exists or cannot be created. mode defaults to 0o777 (octal). In Python 3.2 and later, this call has an additional optional argument exists_ok; see Python manual.

`os.readlink(path)`

> Returns the path referenced by a symbolic link *path*.

`os.remove(path)`

`os.unlink(path)`

> Removes (deletes) the file named *path*. remove() is identical to unlink(). See also rmdir() and removedirs() in this list for removing directories.

`os.removedirs(path)`

> Recursive directory-removal function. Similar to rmdir(), but if the leaf directory is successfully removed, directories

corresponding to the rightmost path segments will then be pruned until either the whole path is consumed or an error is raised. Throws an exception if the leaf directory could not be removed.

`os.rename(srcpath, dstpath)`

Renames (moves) file *srcpath* to name *dstpath*. See also `os.replace()` as of Python 3.3 in Python manuals.

`os.renames(oldpath, newpath)`

Recursive directory- or file-renaming function. Like `rename()`, but creation of any intermediate directories needed to make the new pathname valid is attempted first. After the rename, directories corresponding to the rightmost path segments of the old name will be pruned using `removedirs()`.

`os.rmdir(path)`

Removes (deletes) a directory named *path*.

`os.stat(path)`

Runs `stat` system call for *path*; returns a tuple of integers with low-level file information (whose items are defined and processed by tools in standard library module `stat`).

`os.symlink(srcpath, dstpath)`

Creates a symbolic link to file *srcpath*, called *dstpath*.

`os.utime(path, (atime, mtime))`

Sets file *path* access and modification times.

`os.access(path, mode)`

Consult the Python Library Reference or Unix manpages for details.

`os.walk(...)`

```
os.walk(top
    [, topdown=True
    [, onerror=None]
    [, followlinks=False]]])
```

Generates the filenames in a directory tree by walking the tree either top-down or bottom-up. For each directory in the tree rooted at the possibly relative directory path named by string *top* (including *top* itself), yields a three-item tuple (a.k.a. *triple*) (*dirpath, dirnames, filenames*), where:

- *dirpath* is a string, the path to the directory.

- *dirnames* is a list of the names of the subdirectories in *dirpath* (excluding . and ..).

- *filenames* is a list of the names of the nondirectory files in *dirpath*.

Note that the names in the lists do not contain path components. To get a full path (which begins with *top*) to a file or directory in *dirpath*, run os.path.join(*dirpath, name*).

If optional argument topdown is true or not specified, the triple for a directory is generated *before* the triples for any of its subdirectories (directories are generated top-down). If topdown is false, the triple for a directory is generated *after* the triples for all its subdirectories (directories are generated bottom-up). If optional onerror is specified, it should be a function, which will be called with one argument, an os.error instance. By default, os.walk will not walk down into symbolic links that resolve to directories; set followlinks to True to visit directories pointed to by such links, on systems that support them.

When topdown is true, the *dirnames* list may be modified in-place to control the search, as os.walk() will recurse into only the subdirectories whose names remain in *dirnames*. This is useful to prune the search, impose a specific order of visitations, etc.

Python 2.X also provides an os.path.walk() call with similar tree-walking functionality, using an event-handler function callback instead of a generator. In Python 3.X, os.path.walk() is removed due to its redundancy; use os.walk() instead. See also module glob in Python manuals

for related filename expansion (e.g., glob.glob
(r'***.py')).

Process Control

The following functions are used to create and manage *processes
and programs*. See also "Shell Commands" for other ways to start
programs and files. Hint: do not use these tools to launch untrustworthy shell command strings, as they may run any command allowed for the Python process:

os.abort()
> Sends a SIGABRT signal to the current process. On Unix, the
> default behavior is to produce a core dump; on Windows,
> the process immediately returns exit code 3.

os.execl(*path, arg0, arg1,...*)
> Equivalent to execv(*path,* (*arg0, arg1,...*)).

os.execle(*path, arg0, arg1,..., env*)
> Equivalent to execve(*path,* (*arg0, arg1,...*), *env*).

os.execlp(*path, arg0, arg1,...*)
> Equivalent to execvp(*path,* (*arg0, arg1,...*)).

os.execve(*path, args, env*)
> Like execv(), but the *env* dictionary replaces the shell vari-
> able environment. *env* must map strings to strings.

os.execvp(*path, args*)
> Like execv(*path, args*), but duplicates the shell's actions in
> searching for an executable file in a list of directories. The
> directory list is obtained from os.environ['PATH'].

os.execvpe(*path, args, env*)
> A cross between execve() and execvp(). The directory list
> is obtained from os.environ['PATH'].

os.execv(*path, args*)
> Executes the executable file *path* with the command-line
> argument *args*, replacing the current program in this pro-
> cess (the Python interpreter). *args* can be a tuple or a list of

strings, and it starts with the executable's name by convention (argv[0]). This function call never returns, unless an
error occurs while starting the new program.

os._exit(*n*)

Exits the process immediately with status *n*, without per-
forming normal program termination steps. Normally used
only in a child process after a fork; the standard way to exit
is to call sys.exit(*n*).

os.fork()

Spawns a child process (a virtual copy of the calling process,
running in parallel); returns 0 in the child and the new child's
process ID in the parent. Not available in standard Windows
Python, but is available on Windows in Cygwin Python
(popen(), system(), spawnv(), and the subprocess module
are generally more portable).

os.getpid()

os.getppid()

Returns the process ID of the current (calling) process;
getppid() returns the parent process ID.

os.getuid()

os.geteuid()

Returns the process's user ID; geteuid returns the effective
user ID.

os.kill(*pid, sig*)

Send signal *sig* to the process with ID *pid*, potentially killing
it (for some signal types). See also the signal standard library module in Python manuals for signal constants and
signal handler registration.

os.mkfifo(*path* [, *mode*])

See the earlier section "File Pathname Tools" (named files
used for process synchronization).

os.nice(*increment*)

Adds *increment* to process's "niceness" (i.e., lowers its CPU
priority).

`os.pipe()`

> Returns a tuple of file descriptors (*readfd*, *writefd*) for reading and writing a new anonymous (unnamed) pipe. Used for cross-process communication of related processes.

`os.plock(op)`

> Locks program segments into memory. *op* (defined in `<sys./lock.h>`) determines which segments are locked.

`os.spawnv(mode, path, args)`

> Executes program *path* in a new process, passing the arguments specified in *args* as a command line. *args* can be a list or a tuple. *mode* is an operational constant made from the following names, also defined in the `os` module: `P_WAIT`, `P_NOWAIT`, `P_NOWAITO`, `P_OVERLAY`, and `P_DETACH`. On Windows, roughly equivalent to a `fork()` plus `execv()` combination. (`fork()` is not available on standard Windows Python, although `popen()` and `system()` are.) See also the standard library `subprocess` module for more feature-rich alternatives to this call (see "The subprocess Module").

`os.spawnve(mode, path, args, env)`

> Like `spawnv()`, but passes the contents of mapping *env* as the spawned program's shell environment (else it would inherit its parent's).

`os.wait()`

> Waits for completion of a child process. Returns a tuple with child's ID and exit status.

`os.waitpid(pid, options)`

> Waits for child process with ID *pid* to complete. *options* is 0 for normal use, or `os.WNOHANG` to avoid hanging if no child status is available. If *pid* is 0, the request applies to any child in the process group of the current process. See also the process exit status-check functions documented in the Python Library Reference (e.g., `WEXITSTATUS(status)` to extract the exit code).

The os.path Module

The os.path module provides additional file *directory pathname-related* services and portability tools. This is a nested module: its names are nested in the os module within the submodule os.path (e.g., the exists function may be obtained by importing os and using name os.path.exists).

Most functions in this module take an argument *path*, the string directory pathname of a file (e.g., 'C:\dir1\spam.txt'). Directory paths are generally coded per the platform's conventions and are mapped to the current working directory if lacking a directory prefix. Hint: forward slashes usually work as directory separators on all platforms. In Python 2.X, this module includes an os.path.walk() tool, which has been replaced by os.walk() in Python 3.X (see "File Pathname Tools"):

os.path.abspath(*path*)

>Returns a normalized absolute version of *path*. On most platforms, this is equivalent to normpath(join(os.getcwd(), *path*)).

os.path.basename(*path*)

>Same as second half of pair returned by split(*path*).

os.path.commonprefix(*list*)

>Returns longest path prefix (character by character) that is a prefix of all paths in *list*.

os.path.dirname(*path*)

>Same as first half of pair returned by split(*path*).

os.path.exists(*path*)

>True if string *path* is the name of an existing file path.

os.path.expanduser(*path*)

>Returns string that is *path* with embedded ˜ username expansion done.

os.path.expandvars(*path*)

>Returns string that is *path* with embedded $ environment variables expanded.

`os.path.getatime(path)`
> Returns time of last access of *path* (seconds since the epoch).

`os.path.getmtime(path)`
> Returns time of last modification of *path* (seconds since the epoch).

`os.path.getsize(path)`
> Returns size, in bytes, of file *path*.

`os.path.isabs(path)`
> True if string *path* is an absolute path.

`os.path.isfile(path)`
> True if string *path* is a regular file.

`os.path.isdir(path)`
> True if string *path* is a directory.

`os.path.islink(path)`
> True if string *path* is a symbolic link.

`os.path.ismount(path)`
> True if string *path* is a mount point.

`os.path.join(path1 [, path2 [, ...]])`
> Joins one or more path components intelligently (using platform-specific separator conventions between each part).

`os.path.normcase(path)`
> Normalizes case of a pathname. Has no effect on Unix; on case-insensitive filesystems, converts to lowercase; on Windows, also converts / to \.

`os.path.normpath(path)`
> Normalizes a pathname. Collapses redundant separators and up-level references; on Windows, converts / to \.

`os.path.realpath(path)`
> Returns the canonical path of the specified filename, eliminating any symbolic links encountered in the path.

`os.path.samefile(path1, path2)`

    True if both pathname arguments refer to the same file or directory.

`os.path.sameopenfile(fp1, fp2)`

    True if both file objects refer to the same file.

`os.path.samestat(stat1, stat2)`

    True if both `stat` tuples refer to the same file.

`os.path.split(path)`

    Splits *path* into (*head*, *tail*), where *tail* is the last pathname component and *head* is everything leading up to *tail*. Same as tuple (dirname(*path*), basename(*path*)).

`os.path.splitdrive(path)`

    Splits *path* into a pair ('*drive*:', *tail*) (on Windows).

`os.path.splitext(path)`

    Splits *path* into (*root*, *ext*), where the last component of *root* contains no ., and *ext* is empty or starts with a ..

`os.path.walk(path, visitor, data)`

    An alternative to `os.walk()` in Python 2.X only, and based on directory-handler callback function *visitor* with state *data*, instead of directory generator. Removed in Python 3.X: use `os.walk()`, not `os.path.walk()`.

The re Pattern-Matching Module

The `re` module is the standard regular expression *pattern-matching* interface in both Python 3.X and 2.X. Regular expression (RE) patterns, and the text to be matched by them, are specified as strings. This module must be imported.

Module Functions

The module's top-level interface includes tools to match immediately or precompile patterns, and creates pattern objects (*pobj*) and match objects (*mobj*) defined in subsequent sections:

`re.compile(pattern [, flags])`

Compile an RE *pattern* string into a RE pattern object (*pobj*), for later matching. *flags* (combinable by bitwise | operator) include the following, available at the top-level of the re module:

`re.A` *or* `re.ASCII` *or* `(?a)`

Makes \w, \W, \b, \B, \s, and \S perform ASCII-only matching instead of full Unicode matching. This is meaningful only for Unicode patterns and is ignored for byte patterns. Note that for backward compatibility, the re.U flag still exists (as well as its synonym re.UNICODE and its embedded counterpart, ?u), but these are redundant in Python 3.X since matches are Unicode by default for strings (and Unicode matching isn't allowed for bytes).

`re.I` *or* `re.IGNORECASE` *or* `(?i)`

Case-insensitive matching.

`re.L` *or* `re.LOCALE` *or* `(?L)`

Makes \w, \W, \b, \B, \s, \S, \d, and \D dependent on the current locale (default is Unicode for Python 3.X).

`re.M` *or* `re.MULTILINE` *or* `(?m)`

Matches to each newline, not whole string.

`re.S` *or* `re.DOTALL` *or* `(?s)`

. matches *all* characters, including newline.

`re.U` *or* `re.UNICODE` *or* `(?u)`

Makes \w, \W, \b, \B, \s, \S, \d, and \D dependent on Unicode character properties (new in version 2.0, and superfluous in Python 3.X).

`re.X` *or* `re.VERBOSE` *or* `(?x)`

Ignores whitespace in the pattern, outside character sets.

`re.match(pattern, string[, flags])`

> If zero or more characters at start of *string* match the *pattern* string, returns a corresponding match object instance (*mobj*), or None if no match. *flags* is as in compile().

`re.search(pattern, string[, flags])`

> Scans through *string* for a location matching *pattern*; returns a corresponding match object instance (*mobj*), or None if no match. *flags* is as in compile().

`re.split(pattern, string[, maxsplit=0])`

> Splits *string* by occurrences of *pattern*. If capturing () are used in *pattern*, occurrences of patterns or subpatterns are also returned.

`re.sub(pattern, repl, string[, count=0])`

> Returns string obtained by replacing the (first count) leftmost nonoverlapping occurrences of *pattern* (a string or an RE object) in *string* by *repl*. *repl* can be a string or a function called with a single match object (*mobj*) argument, which must return the replacement string. *repl* can also include sequence escapes \1, \2, etc., to use substrings that match groups, or \0 for all.

`re.subn(pattern, repl, string[, count=0])`

> Same as *sub* but returns a tuple (*new-string, number-of-subs-made*).

`re.findall(pattern, string[, flags])`

> Returns a list of strings giving all nonoverlapping matches of *pattern* in *string*. If one or more groups are present in the pattern, returns a list of groups.

`re.finditer(pattern, string[, flags])`

> Returns an iterable over all nonoverlapping matches for the RE pattern in string (match objects).

`re.escape(string)`

> Returns *string* with all nonalphanumeric characters backslashed, such that they can be compiled as a string literal.

Regular Expression Objects

RE pattern objects (*pobj*) are returned by the re.compile() and have the following attributes, some of which create match objects (*mobj*):

pobj.flags

> The flags argument used when the RE patterns object was compiled.

pobj.groupindex

> Dictionary of {*group-name*: *group-number*} in the pattern.

pobj.pattern

> The pattern string from which the RE pattern object was compiled.

pobj.match(*string* [, *pos* [, *endpos*]])
pobj.search(*string* [, *pos* [, *endpos*]])
pobj.split(*string* [, maxsplit=0])
pobj.sub(*repl*, *string* [, count=0])
pobj.subn(*repl*, *string* [, count=0])
pobj.findall(*string* [, *pos*[, *endpos*]])
pobj.finditer(*string* [, *pos*[, *endpos*]])

> Same as earlier re module functions, but *pattern* is implied, and *pos* and *endpos* give start/end string indexes for the match. The first two may create match objects (*mobj*).

Match Objects

Match objects (*mobj*) are returned by successful match() and search() operations, and have the following attributes (see the Python Library Reference for additional lesser-used attributes omitted here):

mobj.pos, *mobj*.endpos

> Values of pos and endpos passed to search or match.

mobj.re

> RE pattern object whose match or search produced this match object (see its pattern string).

mobj.string

> String passed to match or search.

mobj.group([*g* [, *g*]*)

> Returns substrings that were matched by parenthesized groups in the pattern. Accepts zero or more group *number* or *name* identifiers *g*, implied by patterns (R) and (? P<*name*>R), respectively. If one argument, result is the substring that matched the group whose identifier passed. If multiple arguments, result is a tuple with one matched substring per argument. If no arguments, returns entire matching substring. If any group number is 0, return value is entire matching string; otherwise, returns string matching corresponding parenthesized group. Groups in pattern are numbered 1...N, from left to right.

mobj.groups()

> Returns a tuple of all groups of the match; groups not participating in the match have a value of None.

mobj.groupdict()

> Returns a dictionary containing all the named subgroups of the match, keyed by the subgroup name.

mobj.start([*g*]), *mobj*.end([*g*])

> Indexes of start and end of substring matched by group *g* (or entire matched string, if no *group*). For a match object M, M.string[M.start(*g*):M.end(*g*)] == M.group(*g*).

mobj.span([*g*])

> Returns the tuple (*mobj*.start(*g*), *mobj*.end(*g*)).

mobj.expand(*template*)

> Returns the string obtained by doing backslash substitution on the string *template*, as done by the sub method. Escapes such as \n are converted to the appropriate characters, and numeric back-references (e.g., \1, \2) and named back-references (e.g., \g<1>, \g<name>) are replaced by the corresponding group.

Pattern Syntax

Pattern strings are specified by concatenating forms (see Table 19), as well as by character class escapes (see Table 20). Python character escapes (e.g., \t for tab) can also appear. Pattern strings are matched against text strings, yielding a Boolean match result, as well as grouped substrings matched by subpatterns in parentheses:

```
>>> import re
>>> pobj = re.compile('hello[ \t]*(.*)')
>>> mobj = pobj.match('hello   world!')
>>> mobj.group(1)
'world!'
```

In Table 19, *C* is any character, *R* is any regular expression form in the left column of the table, and *m* and *n* are integers. Each form usually consumes as much of the string being matched as possible, except for the nongreedy forms (which consume as little as possible, as long as the entire pattern still matches the target string).

Table 19. Regular expression pattern syntax

Form	Description
.	Matches any character (including newline if DOTALL flag is specified).
^	Matches start of string (of every line in MULTILINE mode).
$	Matches end of string (of every line in MULTILINE mode).
C	Any nonspecial character matches itself.
R*	Zero or more occurrences of preceding regular expression *R* (as many as possible).
R+	One or more occurrences of preceding regular expression *R* (as many as possible).
R?	Zero or one occurrence of preceding regular expression *R*.
R{*m*}	Matches exactly *m* repetitions of preceding regular expression *R*.

Form	Description
`R{m,n}`	Matches from *m* to *n* repetitions of preceding regular expression *R*.
`R*?`, `R+?`, `R??`, `R{m,n}?`	Same as `*`, `+`, and `?`, but matches as few characters/times as possible; *nongreedy*.
`[...]`	Defines character set; e.g., `[a-zA-Z]` matches all letters (also see Table 20).
`[^...]`	Defines complemented character set: matches if character is not in set.
`\`	Escapes special characters (e.g., `*?+|()`) and introduces special sequences (see Table 20). Due to Python rules, write as `\\` or `r'..\..'`.
`\\`	Matches a literal `\`; due to Python string rules, write as `\\\\` in pattern, or `r'\\'`.
`\number`	Matches the contents of the group of the same number: `r'(.+) \1'` matches `'42 42'`.
`R|R`	Alternative: matches left or right *R*.
`RR`	Concatenation: matches both *R*s.
`(R)`	Matches any RE inside `()`, and delimits a *group* (retains matched substring).
`(?:R)`	Same as `(R)` but doesn't delimit a group.
`(?=R)`	Look-ahead assertion: matches if *R* matches next, but doesn't consume any of the string (e.g., `'X(?=Y)'` matches X if followed by Y).
`(?!R)`	Negative look-ahead assertion: matches if *R* doesn't match next. Negative of `(?=R)`.
`(?P<name>R)`	Matches any RE inside `()` and delimits a named group (e.g., `r'(?P<id>[a-zA-Z_]\w*)'` defines a group named id).
`(?P=name)`	Matches whatever text was matched by the earlier group named *name*.
`(?#...)`	A comment; ignored.

Form	Description
(?letter)	letter is one of a, i, L, m, s, x, or u. Set flag (re.A, re.I, re.L, etc.) for entire RE.
(?<=R)	Positive look-behind assertion: matches if preceded by a match of fixed-width R.
(?<!R)	Negative look-behind assertion: matches if not preceded by a match of fixed-width R.
(?(id/ name)yespatt| nopatt)	Will try to match with pattern yespatt if the group with given id or name exists, else with optional nopatt.

In Table 20, \b, \B, \d, \D, \s, \S, \w, and \W behave differently depending on flags, and defaults to Unicode in Python 3.X, unless ASCII (a.k.a. ?a) is used. Tip: use raw strings (r'\n') to literalize backslashes in Table 20 class escapes.

Table 20. Regular expression pattern special sequences

Sequence	Description
\number	Matches text of the group number (from 1)
\A	Matches only at the start of the string
\b	Empty string at word boundaries
\B	Empty string not at word boundary
\d	Any decimal digit (like [0-9])
\D	Any nondecimal digit character (like [^0-9])
\s	Any whitespace character (like [\t\n\r\f\v])
\S	Any nonwhitespace character (like [^ \t\n\r\f\v])
\w	Any alphanumeric character
\W	Any nonalphanumeric character
\Z	Matches only at the end of the string

Object Persistence Modules

Three modules comprise the standard library's *object persistence* (Python object storage) system:

dbm *(anydbm in Python 2.X)*
> Key-based string-only storage files.

pickle *(and cPickle in Python 2.X)*
> Serializes an in-memory object to/from file streams.

shelve
> Key-based persistent object stores: stores objects in dbm files in pickle form.

The shelve module implements persistent object stores. shelve in turn uses the pickle module to convert (serialize) in-memory Python objects to linear strings and the dbm module to store those linear strings in access-by-key files. All three modules can be used directly.

NOTE

In Python 2.X, dbm is named anydbm, and the cPickle module is an optimized version of pickle that may be imported directly and is used automatically by shelve, if present. In Python 3.X, cPickle is renamed _pickle and is automatically used by pickle if present—it need not be imported directly and is acquired by shelve.

Also note that in Python 3.X the Berkeley DB (a.k.a. bsddb) interface for dbm is no longer shipped with Python itself, but is a third-party open source extension, which must be installed separately if needed (see the Python 3.X Library Reference for resources).

The shelve and dbm Modules

dbm is a simple *access-by-key text file*: strings are stored and fetched by their string keys. The dbm module selects the keyed-access file implementation available in your Python interpreter and presents a dictionary-like API for scripts.

shelve is an *access-by-key object file*: it is used like a simple *dbm* file, except that module name differs, and the stored *value* can be almost any kind of Python object (although *keys* are still strings). In most respects, dbm files and shelves work like *dictionaries* that must be opened before use, and closed after making changes; all mapping operations and some dictionary methods work, and are automatically mapped to external files.

File opens

For shelve, import the library, and call its open() to create a new or open an existing shelve file:

```
import shelve
file = shelve.open(filename
          [, flag='c'
          [, protocol=None
          [, writeback=False]]])
```

For dbm, import the library, and call its open() to create a new or open an existing dbm file. This employs whatever dbm support library is available: dbm.bsd, dbm.gnu, dbm.ndbm, or dbm.dumb (the last being a fallback default always present):

```
import dbm
file = dbm.open(filename
          [, flag='r'
          [, mode]])
```

filename in both shelve and dbm is a relative or absolute string name of an external file where data is stored.

flag is the same in shelve and dbm (shelve passes it on to dbm). It can be 'r' to open an existing database for reading only (dbm default); 'w' to open an existing database for reading and writing;

'c' to create the database if it doesn't exist (shelve default); or 'n', which will always create a new empty database. The dbm.dumb module (used by default in 3.X if no other library is installed) ignores flag—the database is always opened for update and is created if it doesn't exist.

For dbm, the optional mode argument is the Unix mode of the file, used only when the database has to be created. It defaults to octal 0o666.

For shelve, the protocol argument is passed on from shelve to pickle. It gives the pickling protocol number (described in "The pickle Module") used to store shelved objects; it defaults to 0 in Python 2.X, and currently to 3 in Python 3.X.

By default, changes to objects fetched from shelves are not automatically written back to disk. If the optional writeback parameter is set to True, all entries accessed are cached in memory, and written back at close time; this makes it easier to mutate mutable entries in the shelve, but can consume memory for the cache, making the close operation slow because all accessed entries are written back. Reassign objects to their keys to update shelves manually.

File operations

Once created, shelve and dbm have nearly identical, dictionary-like interfaces, as follows:

```
file[key] = value
```

Store: creates or changes the entry for string key. The value is a string for dbm, or a nearly arbitrary object for shelve.

```
value = file[key]
```

Fetch: loads the value for the key entry. For shelve, reconstructs the original object in memory.

```
count = len(file)
```

Size: returns the number of entries stored.

```
index = file.keys()
```

Index: fetches the stored keys iterable (a list in 2.X).

```
for key in file: ...
```

Iterate: keys iterator, usable in any iteration context.

```
found = key in file    # Also has_key() in 2.X only
```

Query: True if there's an entry for *key*.

```
del file[key]
```

Delete: removes the entry for *key*.

```
file.close()
```

Manual close; required to flush updates to disk for some underlying dbm interfaces.

The pickle Module

The pickle module is an *object serialization* tool: it converts nearly arbitrary in-memory Python objects to/from linear bytestreams. These byte-streams can be directed to any file-like object that has the expected read/write methods, and are used by shelve as its internal data representation. Unpickling re-creates the original in-memory object, with the same value, but a new identity (memory address).

See the earlier note about Python 2.X's cPickle and Python 3.X's _pickle optimized modules. Also see the makefile method of socket objects for shipping serialized objects over networks without manual socket calls (see "Internet Modules and Tools" and Python manuals).

Pickling interfaces

This module supports the following calls:

```
P = pickle.Pickler(fileobject [, protocol=None])
```

Makes a new pickler, for saving to an output file object.

```
P.dump(object)
```

Writes an object onto the pickler's file/stream.

```
pickle.dump(object, fileobject [, protocol=None])
```

Combination of the previous two: pickles object onto file.

```
string = pickle.dumps(object [, protocol=None])
```

Returns pickled representation of object as a string (a bytes string in Python 3.X).

Unpickling interfaces

This module supports the following calls:

```
U = pickle.Unpickler(fileobject,
                encoding="ASCII", errors="strict")
```

Makes unpickler, for loading from input file object.

```
object = U.load()
```

Reads object from the unpickler's file/stream.

```
object = pickle.load(fileobject,
                encoding="ASCII", errors="strict")
```

Combination of the previous two: unpickles object from file.

```
object = pickle.loads(string,
                encoding="ASCII", errors="strict")
```

Reads object from a string (a bytes or compatible string in Python 3.X).

pickle usage notes

- In Python 3.X, files used to store pickled objects should always be opened in binary mode for all protocols, because the pickler produces bytes strings, and text mode files do not support writing bytes (text mode files encode and decode Unicode text in 3.X).

- In Python 2.X, files used to store pickled objects must be opened in binary mode for all pickle protocols >= 1, to suppress line-end translations in binary pickled data. Protocol 0 is ASCII-based, so its files may be opened in either text or binary mode, as long as this is done consistently.

- *fileobject* is an open file object, or any object that implements file object attributes called by the interface. Pickler calls the file write() method with a string argument. Unpickler calls the file read() method with a byte-count and readline() without arguments.

- protocol is an optional argument that selects a format for pickled data, available in both the Pickler constructor and the module's dump() and dumps() convenience functions. This argument takes a value 0...3, where higher protocol numbers are generally more efficient, but may also be incompatible with unpicklers in earlier Python releases. The default protocol number in Python 3.X is 3, which cannot be unpickled by Python 2.X. The default protocol in Python 2.X is 0, which is less efficient but most portable. Protocol -1 automatically uses the highest protocol supported. When *unpickling*, protocol is implied by pickled data contents.

- The unpickler's encoding and errors optional keyword-only arguments are available in Python 3.X only. They are used to decode 8-bit string instances pickled by Python 2.X. These default to 'ASCII' and 'strict', respectively. See str() in "Built-in Functions" for similar tools.

- Pickler and Unpickler are exported classes that may be customized by subclassing. See the Python Library Reference for available methods.

The tkinter GUI Module and Tools

`tkinter` (named `Tkinter` in Python 2.X, and a module package in Python 3.X) is a portable *graphical user interface* (GUI) construction library shipped with Python as a standard library module. `tkinter` provides an object-based interface to the open source Tk library and implements native look and feel for Python-coded GUIs on Windows, X-Windows, and Mac OS. It is portable, simple to use, well documented, widely used, mature, and well supported. Other portable GUI options for Python, such as *wxPython* and *PyQT*, are third-party extensions with richer widget sets but generally more complex coding requirements.

tkinter Example

In `tkinter` scripts, *widgets* are customizable classes (e.g., `Button`, `Frame`), *options* are keyword arguments (e.g., `text="press"`), and *composition* refers to object embedding, not pathnames (e.g., `Label(top,...)`):

```python
from tkinter import *          # Widgets, constants

def msg():                     # Callback handler
    print('hello stdout...')

top = Frame()                  # Make a container
top.pack()
Label(top, text='Hello world').pack(side=TOP)
```

```
widget = Button(top, text='press', command=msg)
widget.pack(side=BOTTOM)
top.mainloop()
```

tkinter Core Widgets

Table 21 lists the primary widget classes in the tkinter module. These are Python classes that can be subclassed and embedded in other objects. To create a screen device, make an instance of the corresponding class, configure it, and arrange it with one of the geometry manager interface methods (e.g., Button(text='hello').pack()). In addition to Table 21's classes, the tkinter module provides a large set of predefined names (a.k.a. constants) used to configure widgets (e.g., RIGHT, BOTH, YES); these are automatically loaded from tkinter.constants (Tkconstants in Python 2.X).

Table 21. Module tkinter core widget classes

Widget class	Description
Label	Simple message area
Button	Simple labeled pushbutton widget
Frame	Container for attaching and arranging other widget objects
Toplevel, Tk	Top-level windows managed by the window manager
Message	Multiline text-display field (label)
Entry	Simple single-line text entry field
Checkbutton	Two-state button widget, used for multiple-choice selections
Radiobutton	Two-state button widget, used for single-choice selections
Scale	A slider widget with scalable positions
PhotoImage	Image object for placing full-color images on other widgets
BitmapImage	Image object for placing bitmap images on other widgets
Menu	Options associated with a Menubutton or top-level window
Menubutton	Button that opens a Menu of selectable options/submenus
Scrollbar	Bar for scrolling other widgets (e.g., Listbox, Canvas, Text)

Widget class	Description
Listbox	List of selection names
Text	Multiline text browse/edit widget, support for fonts, etc.
Canvas	Graphics drawing area: lines, circles, photos, text, etc.
OptionMenu	*Composite*: pull-down selection list
PanedWindow	A multipane window interface
LabelFrame	A labeled frame widget
Spinbox	A multiple selection widget
ScrolledText	Python 2.X name (available in module tkinter.scrolledtext in Python 3.X); *Composite*: text with attached scrollbar
Dialog	Python 2.X name (available in module tkinter.dialog in Python 3.X); *Old*: common dialog maker (see newer common dialog calls in the next section)

Common Dialog Calls

Module tkinter.messagebox (tkMessageBox in Python 2.X)

```
showinfo(title=None, message=None, **options)
showwarning(title=None, message=None, **options)
showerror(title=None, message=None, **options)
askquestion(title=None, message=None, **options)
askokcancel(title=None, message=None, **options)
askyesno(title=None, message=None, **options)
askretrycancel(title=None, message=None, **options)
```

Module tkinter.simpledialog (tkSimpleDialog in Python 2.X)

```
askinteger(title, prompt, **kw)
askfloat(title, prompt, **kw)
askstring(title, prompt, **kw)
```

Module tkinter.colorchooser (tkColorChooser in Python 2.X)

```
askcolor(color=None, **options)
```

Module tkinter.filedialog (tkFileDialog in Python 2.X)

```
class Open
class SaveAs
class Directory
askopenfilename(**options)
asksaveasfilename(**options)
askopenfile(mode="r", **options)
asksaveasfile(mode="w", **options)
askdirectory(**options)
```

The common dialog call *options* are defaultextension (added to filename if not explicitly given), filetypes (sequence of (label, pattern) tuples), initialdir (initial directory, remembered by classes), initialfile (initial file), parent (window in which to place the dialog box), and title (dialog box title).

Additional tkinter Classes and Tools

Table 22 lists some commonly used tkinter interfaces and tools beyond the core widget class and standard dialog set. All of these are standard library tools, except some in the last row (e.g., Pillow); see the Web.

Table 22. Additional tkinter tools

Tool category	Available tools
tkinter linked-variable classes	StringVar, IntVar, DoubleVar, Boolean Var (in tkinter module)
Geometry management methods	pack(), grid(), place() widget object methods, plus configuration options in module
Scheduled callbacks	Widget after(), wait(), and update() methods; file I/O callbacks
Other tkinter tools	Clipboard access; bind()/Event low-level event processing widget object methods; widget config() options; modal dialog box support
tkinter extensions	*PMW*: more widgets; *PIL* (a.k.a *Pillow*): images; tree widgets, font support, drag-and-drop, tix widgets, ttk themed widgets, etc.

Tcl/Tk-to-Python/tkinter Mappings

Table 23 compares Python's tkinter API to the base Tk library as exposed by the Tcl language, Tk's now-distant origin. In general, Tcl's command strings map to objects in the Python language. Specifically, in Python's tkinter, the Tk GUI interface differs from Tcl in the following ways:

Creation
> Widgets are created as class instance objects by calling a widget class.

Masters (parents)
> Parents are previously created objects, passed to widget class constructors.

Widget options
> Options are constructor or config() keyword arguments, or indexed keys.

Operations
> Widget operations (actions) become tkinter widget class object methods.

Callbacks
> Callback handlers are any callable object: function, method, lambda, class with __call__ method, etc.

Extension
> Widgets are extended using Python class inheritance mechanisms.

Composition
> Interfaces are constructed by attaching objects, not by concatenating names.

Linked variables
> Variables associated with widgets are tkinter class objects with methods.

Table 23. Tk-to-tkinter mappings

Operation	Tcl/Tk	Python/tkinter
Creation	`frame .panel`	`panel = Frame()`
Masters	`button .panel.quit`	`quit = Button(panel)`
Options	`button .panel.go - fg black`	`go = Button(panel, fg='black')`
Configure	`.panel.go config - bg red`	`go.config(bg='red') go['bg'] = 'red'`
Actions	`.popup invoke`	`popup.invoke()`
Packing	`pack .panel -side left -fill x`	`panel.pack(side=LEFT, fill=X)`

Internet Modules and Tools

This section summarizes Python's support for *Internet scripting* in Python 3.X and 2.X. It gives brief overviews of some of the more commonly used modules in the Python standard library's Internet modules set. *This is just a representative sample*; see the Python Library Reference for a more complete list:

socket
> Low-level network communications support (TCP/IP, UDP, etc.). Interfaces for sending and receiving data over BSD-style sockets: socket.socket() makes an object with socket call methods (e.g., *object*.bind()). Most protocol and server modules use this module internally.

socketserver (SocketServer *in Python 2.X*)
> Framework for general threading and forking network servers.

xdrlib
> Encodes binary data portably (also see socket modules earlier in this list).

select

Interfaces to Unix and Windows select() function. Waits for activity on one of a set of files or sockets. Commonly used to multiplex among multiple streams or to implement time-outs. Works only for sockets on Windows, not files.

cgi

Server-side CGI script support: cgi.FieldStorage() parses the input stream; cgi.escape() (and html.escape() in recent 3.X) applies HTML escape conventions to output streams. To parse and access form information: after a CGI script calls *form*=cgi.FieldStorage(), *form* is a dictionary-like object with one entry per form field (e.g., *form*["name"].value is form's name field text).

urllib.request (urllib, urllib2 *in Python 2.X*)

Fetches web pages and server script outputs from their Internet addresses (URLs): urllib.request.urlopen(*url*) returns a file-like object with read methods; also urllib.request.urlretrieve(*remote*, *local*). Supports HTTP, HTTPS, FTP, and local file URLs.

urllib.parse (urlparse *in Python 2.X*)

Parses URL string into components. Also contains tools for escaping URL text: urllib.parse.quote_plus(*str*) does URL escapes for text inserted into HTML output streams.

ftplib

FTP (file transfer protocol) modules. ftplib provides interfaces for Internet file transfers in Python programs. After *ftp*=ftplib.FTP('*sitename*'), *ftp* has methods for login, changing directories, fetching/storing files and listings, etc. Supports binary and text transfers; works on any machine with Python and a usable Internet connection.

poplib, imaplib, smtplib

POP, IMAP (mail fetch), and SMTP (mail send) protocol modules.

`email` *package*

> Parses and constructs email messages with headers and attachments. Also contains MIME support for both content and headers.

`http.client` (`httplib` *in Python 2.X*), `nntplib`, `telnetlib`

> HTTP (web), NNTP (news), and Telnet protocol client modules.

`http.server` (`CGIHTTPServer`, `SimpleHTTPServer` *in Python 2.X*)

> HTTP request server implementations.

`xml` *package*, `html` *package* (`htmllib` *in Python 2.X*)

> Parse XML and HTML documents and web page contents. `xml` package supports DOM, SAX, and ElementTree parsing models, with Expat parsing.

`xmlrpc` *package* (`xmlrpclib` *in Python 2.X*)

> XML-RPC remote method call protocol.

`uu`, `binhex`, `base64`, `binascii`, `quopri`

> Encodes and decodes binary (or other) data transmitted as text.

Table 24 lists some of these modules by protocol type; see the preceding list for 2.X names that differ.

Table 24. Selected Python 3.X Internet modules by protocol

Protocol	Common function	Port number	Python module
HTTP	Web pages	80	`http.client`, `urllib.request`, `xmlrpc.*`
NNTP	Usenet news	119	`nntplib`
FTP data default	File transfers	20	`ftplib`, `urllib.request`
FTP control	File transfers	21	`ftplib`, `urllib.request`
SMTP	Sending email	25	`smtplib`

Protocol	Common function	Port number	Python module
POP3	Fetching email	110	`poplib`
IMAP4	Fetching email	143	`imaplib`
Telnet	Command lines	23	`telnetlib`

Other Standard Library Modules

This section documents a handful of additional standard library modules installed with Python itself. Unless otherwise noted, tools covered here apply to both Python 3.X and 2.X. See the Python Library Reference for details on all built-in tools, and the PyPI website (described in "Assorted Hints") or your favorite web search engine for third-party modules and tools.

The math Module

The `math` module exports C standard *math library tools* for use in Python. Table 25 lists this module's exports in Python 3.3, with seven recent additions in 3.2 and 3.3 in bold font. Python 2.7's module is identical, but has no `log2` or `isfinite`. Contents of this table may vary slightly in other releases. All its entries are callable functions (with trailing parentheses omitted here), except for `pi` and `e`.

For more details, see the Python Library Reference, or import `math` and run `help(math.name)` for arguments and notes for any name in this table, and `dir(math)` to see module content. Also see the `cmath` standard library module for complex number tools, and the *NumPy* third-party system (and others) on the Web for advanced numeric work.

Table 25. math module exports in Python 3.3

acos	acosh	asin	asinh	atan
atan2	atanh	ceil	copysign	cos
cosh	degrees	e	**erf**	**erfc**
exp	**expm1**	fabs	factorial	floor
fmod	frexp	fsum	**gamma**	hypot
isfinite	isinf	isnan	ldexp	**lgamma**
log	log10	log1p	**log2**	modf
pi	pow	radians	sin	sinh
sqrt	tan	tanh	trunc	

The time Module

Utilities related to *time and date*: time access, formatting, and pauses. Following is a partial list of time module exports. See also "The datetime Module", "The timeit Module", and the Python Library Reference for more details:

time.clock()

> Returns the CPU time or real time since the start of the process or since the first call to clock(). Precision and semantics are platform-dependent (see Python manuals). Returns seconds expressed as a floating-point number. Useful for benchmarking and timing alternative code sections.

time.time()

> Returns a floating-point number representing UTC time in seconds since the epoch. On Unix, epoch is 1970. May have better precision than clock() on some platforms (see Python manuals).

time.ctime(*secs*)

> Converts a time expressed in seconds since the epoch to a string representing local time (e.g., ctime(time())). The argument is optional and defaults to the current time if omitted.

```
time.sleep(secs)
```
Suspends the process's (calling thread's) execution for *secs* seconds. *secs* can be a float to represent fractions of seconds.

The next two calls are available in *Python 3.3* and later only. They are designed to provide timing data portably (but may not be directly comparable with calls in earlier Python versions). For both, the reference point of the returned value is undefined, so that only the difference between the results of consecutive calls is valid:

```
time.perf_counter()
```
Returns the value in fractional seconds of a performance counter, defined as a clock with the highest available resolution to measure a short duration. It includes time elapsed during sleep states and is systemwide. Can be thought of as wall time, and if present, is used by default in the timeit module.

```
time.process_time()
```
Returns the value in fractional seconds of the sum of the system and user CPU time of the current process. It does not include time elapsed during sleep, and is process-wide by definition.

The timeit Module

Tools for portably *measuring execution time* of a code string or function call. See Python's manuals for complete details.

Command-line interface:

```
py[thon] -m timeit [-n number] [-r repeat]
         [-s setup]* [-t] [-c] [-p] [-h] [statement]*
```

Where *number* is times to run statements (default is a computed power of 10); *repeat* is runs to make (default 3); *setup* (zero or more, each with -s) is code to run before timed statements; *statement* (zero or more) is the code to be timed; -h prints help; and -t, -c, and -p specify timers to use—time.time(), time.clock(), or as of Python 3.3 time.process_time() (else time.perf_counter() is the default in 3.3 and later). Displayed results give the best time among the *repeat* runs made, which helps neutralize transient system load fluctuations.

Library API interface:

```
timeit.Timer(stmt='pass', setup='pass', timer=dflt)
```

Used by the following convenience functions. Both stmt and setup are either a code string (use ; or \n to separate multiple statements, and spaces or \t for indentation), or a no-argument callable. The timer function's default, *dflt*, is platform and version-dependent.

```
timeit.repeat(stmt='pass', setup='pass',
              timer=dflt, repeat=3, number=1000000)
```

Creates a Timer instance with the given stmt and setup code and timer function, and runs its repeat method with repeat count and number executions. Returns list of timing results: take its min() for best of repeat times.

```
timeit.timeit(stmt='pass', setup='pass',
              timer=dflt, number=1000000)
```

Creates a Timer instance with the given stmt and setup code and timer function and run its timeit method with number executions. Runs setup once; returns time to run stmt number times.

The datetime Module

Tools for *date processing*: subtracting dates, adding days to dates, and so on. See also "The time Module", and the Python Library Reference for more tools and details.

```
>>> from datetime import date, timedelta
>>> date(2013, 11, 15) - date(2013, 10, 29)  # Between
datetime.timedelta(17)

>>> date(2013, 11, 15) + timedelta(60)        # Future
datetime.date(2014, 1, 14)
>>> date(2013, 11, 15) - timedelta(410)       # Past
datetime.date(2012, 10, 1)
```

The random Module

Assorted *randomization* calls: random numbers, shuffles, and selections. See Python manuals for full details.

```
>>> import random
>>> random.random()              # Random float in [0, 1)
0.7082048489415967
>>> random.randint(1, 10)        # Random int in [x, y]
8
>>> L = [1, 2, 3, 4]
>>> random.shuffle(L)            # Shuffle L in place
>>> L
[2, 1, 4, 3]
>>> random.choice(L)             # Choose random item
4
```

The json Module

Utilities for translating Python dictionary and list structures to and from JSON text—a portable *data representation format*, used by systems such as MongoDB (per BSON), and Android's SL4A (in JSON-RPC). See also Python's native object serialization in "The pickle Module"; XML support in "Internet Modules and Tools"; and other database concepts in "Python SQL Database API".

```
>>> R = {'job': ['dev', 1.5], 'emp': {'who': 'Bob'}}

>>> import json
>>> json.dump(R, open('savejson.txt', 'w'))
>>> open('savejson.txt').read()
'{"emp": {"who": "Bob"}, "job": ["dev", 1.5]}'
>>> json.load(open('savejson.txt'))
{'emp': {'who': 'Bob'}, 'job': ['dev', 1.5]}

>>> R = dict(title='PyRef5E', pub='orm', year=2014)
>>> J = json.dumps(R, indent=4)
>>> P = json.loads(J)
>>> P
{'year': 2014, 'title': 'PyRef5E', 'pub': 'orm'}
>>> print(J)
```

```
{
    "year": 2014,
    "title": "PyRef5E",
    "pub": "orm"
}
```

The subprocess Module

Tools for running *command lines*, tapping into any of their three streams, fetching exit codes, and specifying shell execution, which are alternatives to some os module tools such as os.popen() and os.spawnv(); see "The os System Module" and Python manuals for further details. Hint: do not use these tools to launch untrustworthy shell command strings, as they may run any command allowed for the Python process. In the following, script *m.py* prints its sys.argv command line:

```
>>> from subprocess import call, Popen, PIPE
>>> call('python m.py -x', shell=True)
['m.py', '-x']
0
>>> pipe = Popen('python m.py -x', stdout=PIPE)
>>> pipe.communicate()
(b"['m.py', '-x']\r\n", None)
>>> pipe.returncode
0
>>> pipe = Popen('python m.py -x', stdout=PIPE)
>>> pipe.stdout.read()
b"['m.py', '-x']\r\n"
>>> pipe.wait()
0
```

The enum Module

Available as of Python 3.4, this module provides standard support for *enumerations*—sets of symbolic names (a.k.a. *members*) bound to unique, constant values. Not to be confused with the enumerate() call, used to sequentially number iterator results (see "Built-in Functions"):

```
>>> from enum import Enum
>>> class PyBooks(Enum):
```

```
            Learning5E = 2013
            Programming4E = 2011
            PocketRef5E = 2014

>>> print(PyBooks.PocketRef5E)
PyBooks.PocketRef5E
>>> PyBooks.PocketRef5E.name,
    PyBooks.PocketRef5E.value
('PocketRef5E', 2014)

>>> type(PyBooks.PocketRef5E)
<enum 'PyBooks'>
>>> isinstance(PyBooks.PocketRef5E, PyBooks)
True
>>> for book in PyBooks: print(book)
...
PyBooks.Learning5E
PyBooks.Programming4E
PyBooks.PocketRef5E

>>> bks = Enum('Books', 'LP5E PP4E PR5E')
>>> list(bks)
[<Books.LP5E: 1>, <Books.PP4E: 2>, <Books.PR5E: 3>]
```

The struct Module

The struct module provides an interface for parsing and constructing *packed binary data* as strings, per formats designed to mirror C language struct layouts. Often used in conjunction with the 'rb' and 'wb' binary files modes of open(), or other binary data source. See the Python Library Reference for *format* datatype and endian codes.

string = struct.pack(*format*, *v1*, *v2*, ...)

Returns a *string* (a bytes in 3.X and a str in 2.X) containing the values *v1*, *v2*, etc., packed according to the given *format* string. The arguments must match the values required by the *format* string's type codes exactly. The *format* string can specify the endian format of the result in its first character, as well as repeat counts for individual type codes.

```
tuple = struct.unpack(format, string)
```
Unpacks the *string* (a bytes in 3.X and a str in 2.X) into a tuple of Python object values, according to the given *format* string.

```
struct.calcsize(format)
```
Returns size of the struct (and hence of the byte string) corresponding to the given *format*.

Following is an example showing how to pack and unpack data using struct in Python 3.X (Python 2.X uses normal str strings instead of bytes; Python 3.X requires bytes for s values as of 3.2, not str; and '4si' in the following means the same as C's char[4]+int):

```
>>> import struct
>>> data = struct.pack('4si', b'spam', 123)
>>> data
b'spam{\x00\x00\x00'
>>> x, y = struct.unpack('4si', data)
>>> x, y
(b'spam', 123)

>>> open('data', 'wb').write(
                        struct.pack('>if', 1, 2.0))
8
>>> open('data', 'rb').read()
b'\x00\x00\x00\x01@\x00\x00\x00'
>>> struct.unpack('>if', open('data', 'rb').read())
(1, 2.0)
```

Threading Modules

Threads are lightweight processes that share global memory (i.e., scopes, objects, and system internals) and *run functions in parallel* (concurrently) within the same process. Python thread modules work portably across platforms. They are suited for running nonblocking tasks in IO-bound and user-interface contexts.

See also setcheckinterval() and setswitchinterval() in "The sys Module", as well as the multiprocessing standard library

---

module which implements a threading-like API for portably spawned processes:

_thread *(named* thread *in Python 2.X)*

> Basic and low-level thread module, with tools to start, stop, and synchronize functions run in parallel. To spawn a thread: _thread.start_new_thread(*function*, args [, *kargs*]) runs *function* in a new thread, with positional arguments from tuple *args*, and keyword arguments from dictionary *kargs*. start_new_thread is a synonym for start_new (which is documented as obsolete in 3.X). To synchronize threads, use thread locks: *lock*=thread. allocate_lock(); *lock*.acquire(); *update-objects*; *lock*.release().

threading

> Module threading builds upon thread to provide customizable threading-oriented tools: Thread, Condition, Semaphore, Lock, Timer, daemonic threads, thread joins (waits), etc. Subclass Thread to overload run action method. This is functionally richer than _thread, but also requires more code in simpler use cases.

queue *(named* Queue *in Python 2.X)*

> A multiproducer, multiconsumer FIFO queue of Python objects, especially useful for threaded applications. Automatically locks its get() and put() operations to synchronize access to data on the queue. See the Python Library Reference.

Python SQL Database API

Python's portable SQL-based *relational database* API provides script portability between different vendor-specific SQL database packages. For each vendor, install the vendor-specific extension module, but write your scripts according to the portable database API. Your standard SQL database scripts will largely continue working unchanged after migrating to a different underlying vendor package.

Note that most database extension modules are not part of the Python standard library; they are *third-party* components that must be fetched and installed separately. Exception: the SQLite embedded in-process relational database package is included with Python as *standard library* module sqlite3, intended for program data storage and prototyping.

See also "Object Persistence Modules" for simpler storage alternatives. There are additional popular database tools in the third-party domain, including *MongoDB*'s JSON document storage; object-oriented databases such as *ZODB* and others; object-relational mappers including *SQLAlchemy* and *SQLObject*; and cloud-oriented APIs such as *App Engine*'s data store.

API Usage Example

The following uses the SQLite standard library module, and omits some return values for space. Usage for enterprise-level database such as MySQL, PostgreSQL, and Oracle are similar, but require different connection parameters and installation of extension modules, and may support vendor-specific (and nonportable) SQL extensions:

```
>>> from sqlite3 import connect
>>> conn = connect(r'C:\code\temp.db')
>>> curs = conn.cursor()

>>> curs.execute('create table emp (who, job, pay)')
>>> prefix = 'insert into emp values '
>>> curs.execute(prefix + "('Bob', 'dev', 100)")
>>> curs.execute(prefix + "('Sue', 'dev', 120)")

>>> curs.execute("select * from emp where pay > 100")
>>> for (who, job, pay) in curs.fetchall():
...     print(who, job, pay)
...
Sue dev 120

>>> result = curs.execute("select who, pay from emp")
>>> result.fetchall()
[('Bob', 100), ('Sue', 120)]
```

```
>>> query = "select * from emp where job = ?"
>>> curs.execute(query, ('dev',)).fetchall()
[('Bob', 'dev', 100), ('Sue', 'dev', 120)]
```

Module Interface

This and the following sections provide a *partial* list of exports;
see the full API specification at *http://www.python.org* for details
omitted here. Tools at the top-level of the interface module
(*dbmod*):

dbmod.connect(*parameters...*)

>Constructor for a connection object (*conn*) that represents
a connection to the database. Parameters are vendor-
specific.

dbmod.paramstyle

>String giving type of parameter marker formatting (e.g.,
qmark = ? style).

dbmod.Warning

>Exception raised for important warnings, such as data trun-
cations.

dbmod.Error

>Exception that is the base class of all other error exceptions.

Connection Objects

Connection objects (*conn*) respond to the following methods:

conn.close()

>Closes the connection now (rather than when __del__ is
called).

conn.commit()

>Commits any pending transactions to the database.

```
conn.rollback()
```
Rolls database back to the start of any pending transaction; closing a connection without committing the changes first will cause an implicit rollback.

```
conn.cursor()
```
Returns a new cursor object (*curs*) for submitting SQL strings through the connection.

Cursor Objects

Cursor objects (*curs*) represent database cursors, used to manage the context of a fetch operation:

```
curs.description
```
Sequence of seven-item sequences; each contains information describing one result column: (*name*, *type_code*, *display_size*, *internal_size*, *precision*, *scale*, *null_ok*).

```
curs.rowcount
```
Specifies the number of rows that the last execute* variant produced (for DQL statements like select) or affected (for DML statements like update or insert).

```
curs.callproc(procname [, parameters])
```
Calls a stored database procedure with the given name. The sequence of parameters must contain one entry for each argument that the procedure expects; result is returned as a modified copy of the inputs.

```
curs.close()
```
Closes the cursor now (rather than when __del__ is called).

```
curs.execute(operation [, parameters])
```
Prepares and executes a database operation (query or command); parameters can be specified as a list of tuples to insert multiple rows in a single operation (but executemany() is preferred).

`curs.executemany(operation, seq_of_parameters)`

Prepares a database operation (query or command) and executes it against all parameter sequences or mappings in sequence `seq_of_parameters`. Similar to multiple `execute()` calls.

`curs.fetchone()`

Fetches the next row of a query result set, returning a single sequence, or None when no more data is available. Useful for large data sets or slow delivery speed.

`curs.fetchmany([size=curs.arraysize])`

Fetches the next set of rows of a query result, returning a sequence of sequences (e.g., a list of tuples). An empty sequence is returned when no more rows are available.

`curs.fetchall()`

Fetches all (or all remaining) rows of a query result, returning them as a sequence of sequences (e.g., a list of tuples).

Type Objects and Constructors

`Date(year, month, day)`

Constructs an object holding a date value.

`Time(hour, minute, second)`

Constructs an object holding a time value.

`None`

SQL NULL values are represented by the Python None on input and output.

More Hints and Idioms

This section briefly gives common Python coding patterns and usage hints, beyond those disclosed throughout this book. Consult the Python Library Reference and Python Language Reference (*http://www.python.org/doc/*) and the Web at large for further information on some topics mentioned here.

Core Language Hints

- `S[:]` makes a top-level (shallow) copy of any sequence; `copy.deepcopy(X)` makes full copies; `list(L)` and `D.copy()` copy lists and dictionaries (also `L.copy()` for lists as of 3.3).

- `L[:0]=iterable` inserts multiple items in *iterable* at front of list *L*, in-place.

- `L[len(L):]=iterable`, `L.extend(iterable)`, and `L+=iterable` all insert multiple items in *iterable* at the end of a list *L*, in-place.

- `L.append(X)` and `X=L.pop()` can be used to implement in-place stack operations, where *X* is stacked items, and the end of the list is the top of the stack.

- Use `for key in D.keys()` to iterate through dictionaries, or simply `for key in D` in version 2.2 and later. In Python 3.X, these two forms are equivalent, since `keys()` returns an iterable view.

- Use `for key in sorted(D)` to iterate over dictionary keys in sorted fashion in version 2.4 and later; the form `K=D.keys(); K.sort(); for key in K:` also works in Python 2.X but not Python 3.X, since `keys()` results are view objects, not lists.

- `X=A or B or None` assigns *X* to the first true object among *A* and *B*, or else `None` if both are false (i.e., 0 or empty).

- `X,Y = Y,X` swaps the values of *X* and *Y* without requiring assignment of *X* to an explicit temporary.

- `red, green, blue = range(3)` assigns integer series as a simple name enumeration; class attributes and dictionaries may also suffice as enumerations. In Python 3.4 and later, see the more explicit and functionally rich support of enumerations in the `enum` standard library module.

- Use `try`/`finally` statements to ensure that arbitrary termination code is run; especially useful around locked operations (e.g., acquire a lock before the `try`, and release it in the `finally` block).

- Use `with`/`as` statements to guarantee that object-specific termination code is run for objects that support the context manager protocol only (e.g., file auto-close, thread lock auto-release).

- Wrap iterables in a `list()` call to view all their results interactively in Python 3.X, and to ensure that multiple traversals work properly; this includes `range()`, `map()`, `zip()`, `filter()`, `dict.keys()`, and more.

Environment Hints

- Use `if __name__ == '__main__':` to add self-test code or a call to a main function at the bottom of module files; true only when a file is run, not when it is imported as a library component.

- To load file contents in a single expression, use `data=open(filename).read()`. Outside CPython, explicit close calls may be required to force immediate reclamation of system resources (e.g., within loops).

- To iterate through text files by lines, use `for line in file` in version 2.2 and later. (In older versions, use `for line in file.xreadlines()`.)

- To retrieve command-line arguments, use `sys.argv`.

- To access shell environment settings, use `os.environ`.

- The standard streams are: `sys.stdin`, `sys.stdout`, and `sys.stderror`.

- To return a list of files matching a given pattern, use: `glob.glob(pattern)`.

- To return a list of files and subdirectories on a path (e.g., "."), use: os.listdir(*path*).

- To walk an entire tree of directories, use os.walk() in Python 3.X and 2.X. (os.path.walk() is also available in Python 2.X only.)

- To run shell commands within Python scripts, you can use os.system(*cmdline*), *output*=os.popen(*cmdline*, 'r').read(). The latter form reads the spawned program's standard output, and may also be used to read line-by-line and interleave operations.

- Other streams of a spawned command are available via the subprocess module in both Python 3.X and 2.X, and the os.popen2/3/4() calls in Python 2.X only. The os.fork()/os.exec*() calls have similar effect on Unix-like platforms.

- To make a file an executable script on Unix-like platforms, add a line like #!/usr/bin/env python or #!/usr/local/bin/python at the top and give the file executable permissions with a chmod command.

- On Windows, files can be clicked and run directly due to registered filename associations. As of 3.3, the Windows launcher also recognizes #! Unix-style lines: see "Python Windows Launcher Usage".

- print() and input() (known as print and raw_input() in Python 2.X) use sys.stdout and sys.stdin streams: assign to file-like objects to redirect I/O internally, or use the print(..., file=*F*) form in Python 3.X (or the print >> *F*, ... form in Python 2.X).

- Set environment variable PYTHONIOENCODING to utf8 (or other) if your scripts fail when printing non-ASCII Unicode text, such as file names and content.

Usage Hints

- Use `from __future__ import` *featurename* to enable pending language changes that might break existing code, but enable version compatibility.

- Intuition about performance in Python programs is usually wrong: always measure before optimizing or migrating to C. Use the `profile`, `time`, and `timeit` modules (as well as `cProfile`).

- See modules `unittest` (a.k.a. *PyUnit*) and `doctest` for automated testing tools shipped with the Python standard library; `unittest` is a sophisticated class framework; `doctest` scans documentation strings for tests and outputs to rerun interactive sessions.

- The `dir([`*object*`])` function is useful for inspecting attribute namespaces; `print(`*object*`.__doc__)` gives raw docstring documentation.

- The `help([`*object*`])` function provides interactive help for modules, functions, types, type methods, and more; `help(str)` gives help on the `str` type; `help('`*module*`')` gives help on modules even if they have not yet been imported; and `help('`*topic*`')` gives help on keywords and other help topics (use `'topics'` for a list of help topics).

- See *PyDoc*'s `pydoc` library module and script shipped with Python for extraction and display of documentation strings associated with modules, functions, classes, and methods; `python -m pydoc -b` launches PyDoc's browser-based interface as of 3.2 (else use `-g` instead of `-b` for GUI client mode).

- See "Warnings Framework", as well as `-W` in "Python Command Options", for details about turning off future-deprecation warnings emitted by the interpreter.

- See *Distutils*, *eggs*, the next bullet's items, and others for Python program distribution options.

- See *PyInstaller*, *py2exe*, *cx_freeze*, *py2app*, and others for packaging Python programs as standalone executables (e.g., *.exe* files for Windows).

- See *NumPy*, *SciPy*, *Sage*, and related packages for extensions that turn Python into a numeric or scientific-programming tool with vector objects, mathematical libraries, etc. Also watch for the new basic `statistics` standard library module in Python 3.4.

- See *ZODB* and others for full-featured OODB support that allows Python native objects to be stored by key, and *SQLObject*, *SQLAlchemy*, and others for object relational mappers that allow classes to be used with relational tables. See *MongoDB* for a JSON-based "NoSQL" database option.

- See *Django*, *App Engine*, *Web2py*, *Zope*, *Pylons*, *Turbo-Gears*, and others for Python Web development frameworks.

- See *SWIG* (among others) for a tool that can automatically generate glue code for using C and C++ libraries within Python scripts.

- See *IDLE* for a development GUI shipped with Python, with syntax-coloring text editors, object browsers, debugging, etc.; see also *PythonWin*, *Komodo*, *Eclipse*, *NetBeans*, and others for additional IDE options.

- See *Emacs* help for tips on editing/running code in the Emacs text editor. Most other editors support Python as well (e.g., auto-indenting, coloring), including *VIM* and *IDLE*; search for the Python editors' page at *http://www.python.org*.

- Porting to Python 3.X: use the –3 command-line option in Python 2.X to issue incompatibility warnings, and see the *2to3* script, which automatically converts much 2.X code to run under 3.X Python. See also *six*, a system which provides a 2.X/3.X compatibility layer; *3to2*, which aspires to convert 3.X code to run on 2.X interpreters; and *pies*, which also promotes line compatibility.

Assorted Hints

- Relevant websites to refer to:

  http://www.python.org
  > The Python home page

  http://oreilly.com
  > The publisher's home page

  http://www.python.org/pypi
  > Additional third-party Python tools

  http://www.rmi.net/~lutz
  > The author's book support site

- Python philosophy: `import this`.
- You should say `spam` and `eggs` instead of `foo` and `bar` in Python examples.
- Always look on the bright side of life.

Index

We'd like to hear your suggestions for improving our indexes. Send email to index@oreilly.com.

The information you need, when and where you need it.

With Safari Books Online, you can:

Access the contents of thousands of technology and business books

- Quickly search over 7000 books and certification guides
- Download whole books or chapters in PDF format, at no extra cost, to print or read on the go
- Copy and paste code
- Save up to 35% on O'Reilly print books
- **New!** Access mobile-friendly books directly from cell phones and mobile devices

Stay up-to-date on emerging topics before the books are published

- Get on-demand access to evolving manuscripts.
- Interact directly with authors of upcoming books

Explore thousands of hours of video on technology and design topics

- Learn from expert video tutorials
- Watch and replay recorded conference sessions

safaribooksonline.com

O'REILLY®

Get even more for your money.

Join the O'Reilly Community, and register the O'Reilly books you own. It's free, and you'll get:

- $4.99 ebook upgrade offer
- 40% upgrade offer on O'Reilly print books
- Membership discounts on books and events
- Free lifetime updates to ebooks and videos
- Multiple ebook formats, DRM FREE
- Participation in the O'Reilly community
- Newsletters
- Account management
- 100% Satisfaction Guarantee

Signing up is easy:

1. Go to: oreilly.com/go/register
2. Create an O'Reilly login.
3. Provide your address.
4. Register your books.

Note: English-language books only

To order books online:
oreilly.com/store

For questions about products or an order:
orders@oreilly.com

To sign up to get topic-specific email announcements and/or news about upcoming books, conferences, special offers, and new technologies:
elists@oreilly.com

For technical questions about book content:
booktech@oreilly.com

To submit new book proposals to our editors:
proposals@oreilly.com

O'Reilly books are available in multiple DRM-free ebook formats. For more information:
oreilly.com/ebooks

CPSIA information can be obtained at www.ICGtesting.com
Printed in the USA
BVOW08n1609120415

395725BV00006B/10/P